QUILTING

150 Patterns &
Techniques for Machine Stitching

Maggie Malone

 Sterling Publishing Co., Inc.   New York

Edited and designed by Barbara Busch

Library of Congress Cataloging in Publication Data

Malone, Maggie, 1942–
   Quilting : patterns and techniques for machine
stitching.

   Includes index.
   1. Machine quilting.   I. Title.
TT835.M356   1985   746.46   84-23998
ISBN 0-8069-5706-9
ISBN 0-8069-7986-0 (pbk.)

CONTENTS

INTRODUCTION

Quilting is an ancient technique whose origins are lost in the mists of time. It probably developed shortly after weaving was perfected, when it was found that two layers of cloth provided greater warmth than one. These early quilts may have been tied with short lengths of fibre to keep them together. However it started, we do know that the Egyptians practiced quilting as can be seen in their hieroglyphics. There are also surviving scraps of quilted cloth that were made 3,000 years ago.

The use of quilted cloth and clothing was widespread throughout Asia and the Middle East, but it did not develop in Europe until the Crusaders journeyed to the Middle East. There they met warriors fighting in quilted armor and discovered that a quilted jacket under their own armor protected them from the harshness of chain mail.

The first examples of quilted covers in Europe were quite crude, just a few stitches to hold the fabric sandwich together as protection from the cold winters.

The ladies of the fourteenth century, being highly skilled needlewomen, could not long let those vast expanses of fabric remain unadorned. The difficulty of working on the bulky quilts was soon solved by placing them in a frame, somewhat like an oversized embroidery frame, where the fabric could be stretched taut. Now they could comfortably apply intricate embroidery patterns to the surface with a small running stitch.

The highly accomplished needlewomen of Italy developed the trapunto style of quilting. This technique entails stitching to parallel lines, then running cording through the channel formed to give a raised effect to the design. A further development of this type of quilting is stuffed work, where the design is first quilted then certain portions are stuffed with additional padding to make the design stand out.

The colonists in America brought their quilts with them. In the early years the high art of Europe was left behind because there just wasn't time to work the elaborate designs into the quilt tops—not with the cold winters coming on and blankets needed desperately for warmth. These early quilts were whole pieces of cloth, seamed together to the proper size and loosely quilted or even tied to hold them together. By the mid-eighteenth century though, time and material were easier to come by, particularly for upper-class ladies. More elaborate designs were used on their quilts, copying the styles of Europe.

At the same time, adventurous settlers were pushing westward over the Appalachian Mountains into West Virginia, Kentucky and Ohio. The women still had to provide clothing and bedding for their families, but they were developing a whole new style of quilt making. They found it was easier to work a quilt one block at a time rather than to try to find the space for full-sized pieces of cloth. The blocks could be worked in their laps while they travelled overland in wagons or sat by the fire in their small, cramped, one-room cabins. When all the blocks were completed, they were set together to form the quilt top. As before, these early quilts were tied or merely quilted with simple straight lines to hold the layers together.

Again, as life became easier, the quilting became more elaborate, each woman showing off her skill with the needle by filling the quilt with fine, closely quilted designs. I used to object when I heard the statement, "Women don't quilt any more," but after examining some of these old quilts, I can understand the statement. Close quilting was necessary to keep the filler from shifting, but some of these quilts are quilted so closely that there is barely an eighth of an inch between the lines of stitching.

While most of the quilting was done on patch-work quilts, once a woman was sure of her skills, she would attempt an all-quilted quilt. These were embellished with elaborate floral designs, scrolls and feathers, often stuffed to enhance the design. Stuffed work was also used extensively on the alternate plain blocks of a pieced or appliquéd quilt. Stuffed work was even used on appliqué blocks to make certain elements of the design stand out.

While the primary purpose of the quilting stitch is to hold the three layers together, the choice of design and execution of the quilting will greatly enhance the finished quilt. You should spend as much time and care in choosing the quilting design as you did in choosing the pattern for making the quilt top.

Much has been written in recent years about patterns but little on the actual quilting and designs used to finish the quilt. Even the magazines skim over this very important aspect of quilting. This book was written to help fill that gap.

In these pages you will find designs for blocks, borders and small designs for fill taken from my pattern collection. To provide a wider assortment of designs for the modern quilter, I adapted patterns from other craft sources and made up a few of my own. After you've exhausted the designs given here, reread the section on design ideas and make up your own to fit your needs.

THE PRELIMINARIES

CHOOSING A QUILTING DESIGN

Intricate quilting designs, such as the many presented here, are usually used to fill alternate plain blocks and borders, or where you have large areas of unpatterned space to fill because fancy quilt designs will not show up against a patterned background.

For geometric patterns that are set solid, you have many options when it comes to selecting a quilting design.

The simplest choice is outline quilting. Using this method you quilt three-eighths to one-quarter inch on each side of all seam lines. A second method of outline quilting is to quilt "in the ditch," which means directly in the seam line of each piece. You sew only one line of stitching so the quilting is finished faster than when using the double-line quilting.

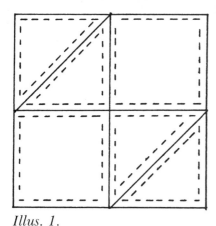

Illus. 1.

If the individual patches of the block are large, leaving more than one to one and a half inches unquilted, you can fill in the pieces with shadow quilting. This consists of repeating the outline quilting in succeeding rows to fill in the area.

In some cases you may want to emphasize the

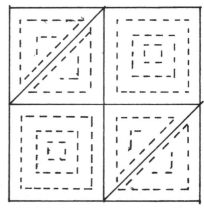

Illus. 2. Shadow quilting.

illusion created by the quilt pattern. Kaleidoscope gives the illusion of large interlocking angular circles when the blocks are joined. To emphasize this design element, quilt around the circles, ignoring the seam lines, then shadow quilt to the center.

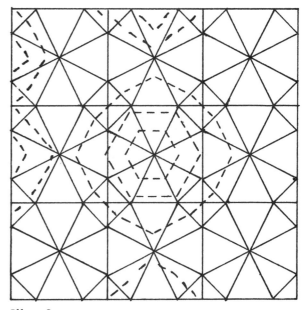

Illus. 3.

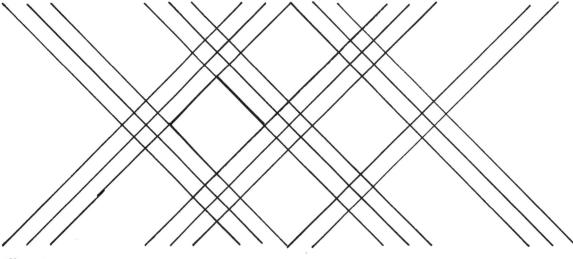

Illus. 4.

Or you can ignore the pattern of the top entirely and use an overall design. The most common design for this purpose is the use of diagonal lines spaced one-half to one inch apart across the quilt top. If you run another line of diagonal lines in the opposite direction, you will have a pattern of diamonds. Although most people seem to find the diamond design more visually exciting, you can also run the lines straight up and down and crosswise to form squares. You might also try multiple lines to form an interesting design as shown in Illus. 4.

A general rule of thumb is that you use straight-line quilting with circular patterns and circular designs with geometric patterns. The geometric design in Illus. 5 shows one of the many possibilities for using circles to enhance a quilt.

Templates for circles can be anything from a cup to a pan lid depending on the size of circle you need. Of course, there's always a compass to fall back on. The clamshell is one of the most popular circle designs but there are many other possibilities. Experiment with different arrangements and sizes until you come up with a pleasing design. Illus. 6–10 provide some ideas to get you started.

Illus. 6.

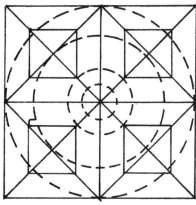

Illus. 5.

You can also create some interesting designs by using hexagons and pentagons.

Many quilt patterns consist of a pieced half set with a solid plain half as in the Sawtooth pattern.

8

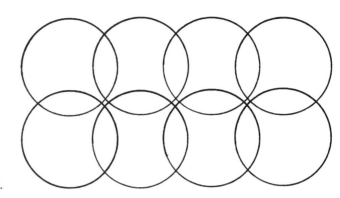

Illus. 7.

Illus. 8.

Illus. 9.

Illus. 10.

The plain half can be quilted using an elaborate motif, and outline quilting can be used for the pieced half, or you could repeat the pieced design on the plain half. This idea will work beautifully on an appliqué quilt set with alternate plain blocks, especially if stuffed quilting is used on the plain blocks to emphasize the design. (See Illus. 11.)

TRANSFERRING THE DESIGN

At present, quilting is enjoying such popularity that new shops are springing up all across the country, which cater to the demand for quilting supplies. Sturdy plastic stencils are available in these shops, and selections range from a few standard feather designs in some to other shops which carry hundreds of different design stencils.

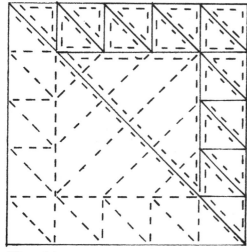

Illus. 11.

Manufacturers are constantly bringing out new items to make the job easier. One manufacturer has recently marketed a quilting stencil that you stick to the fabric, you then quilt around the outline of the design, after which you move the stencil to the next block. No marking is needed.

However, in the future, as in the past, these tools may not be so easy to come by. You also have greater flexibility in your choice of design if you are not confined to ready-made stencils. And it's cheaper to make your own.

If your quilting design is a straight-line, allover pattern, you need nothing more than a ruler and a pencil to mark directly on the fabric. But if you are using a more elaborate design, the marking process becomes a two-step operation. First you must make a working pattern, either a stencil or a perforated pattern sheet. The second step is the actual marking.

MAKING THE PATTERN SHEET

Stencils.* The preferred material for a stencil is a sheet of clear, heavy plastic that is soft enough to cut. Lightweight plastic sheets can be used, but the edges tend to move around when you trace the design onto the fabric. Colored plastic sheets can also be used, but you will have to transfer the design to the plastic before you cut it out.

You will need a sharp craft knife or a double-bladed knife. This type of knife has two blades side by side so that you can cut both sides of the line with one cut. It can be adjusted to varying widths by simply maintaining pressure on the hand grip. Be sure to have extra blades on hand so that you can change them when they start to get dull. Dull blades make the work harder and the lines are not as cleanly cut.

You will also need a sheet of glass large enough to cover the pattern.

Tape your design pattern to the underside of the glass, face up. Tape your clear plastic sheet on top of the glass so you can see your design through it.

Study your design so you can decide where to leave "bridges." These are small areas of uncut plastic that will hold the stencil together. When you start quilting, you ignore the broken line and quilt directly over the bridge.

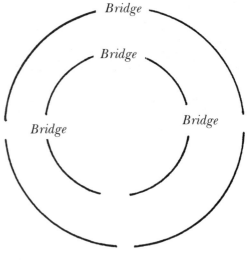

Illus. 12.

*For elaborate designs that will be repeated several times on the quilt top, a stencil is the fastest and easiest method to use.

The best example for the need of a bridge is if you are cutting a series of circles. If a bridge is not left, all the circles will fall out, leaving only the largest one.

Whenever two lines cross, a bridge should be left to stabilize the pattern so that it won't move around when you are tracing it. Long curves should have bridges spaced evenly along the line of the curve, again to prevent movement of the pattern while tracing.

Use a soft-tip marker to place a little line on the areas where you will leave a bridge. With your knife, cut along the line of the pattern between two bridges. Go back and cut the other side of the line and each end. The cut line should be about one-sixteenth of an inch wide, just wide enough for the point of a pencil to move easily. If using a double-bladed knife, adjust the width to one-sixteenth inch and cut along the line, cutting both sides at once. When you reach the end, cut crosswise. Measure over one-eighth inch to allow for the bridge, and continue cutting the line to the next bridge.

A sheet of hard cardboard can be used for a stencil as well as the colored plastic I mentioned before. When using cardboard, use a file folder or something similar. The cardboard used for tablet backs is not suitable because it is very soft and breaks down quickly from the action of the pencil against the edges. If using cardboard or colored plastic, your first step is to transfer the design to the cardboard. You then proceed in the same manner as with a plastic stencil.

PERFORATED PATTERNS

This type of pattern was quite common during the thirties and even earlier. It is not as permanent as a stencil because the paper is subject to wear and tear and it is a bit messy to use since you use chalk to transfer the design to the fabric, but it is quicker and easier to make than a stencil.

Trace the selected design onto a sheet of paper.

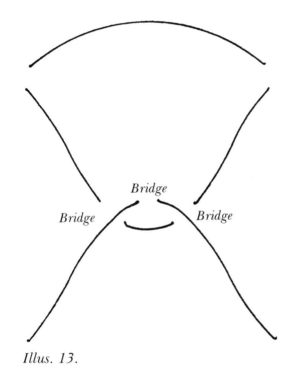

Illus. 13.

Illus. 14.

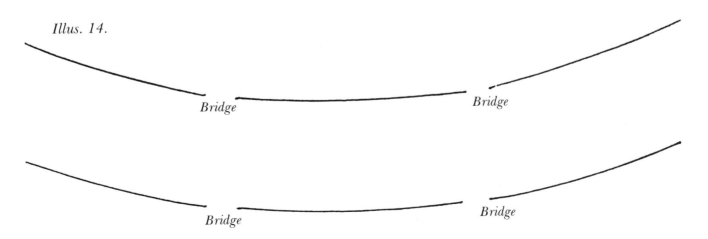

Place the largest needle possible in your sewing machine, then sew over the lines of the design with an unthreaded needle. The design is transferred to the fabric by placing the pattern sheet on the quilt top and pouncing tailor's chalk through the holes with either a powder puff or cotton ball.

If the design consists of long, easy curves, you could use a toothed tracing wheel to punch holes in the pattern. This results in larger holes, making it easier to pounce the chalk through.

Mark small sections at a time, since the chalk tends to rub off during the quilting process.

Once your pattern is completed, you are ready for the actual transfer to the fabric. Easy removal of the lines on the quilt top is your major consideration when choosing a method to use for transferring the design. For those of you who don't like to wash your quilts in the washing machine, it is doubly important that you choose a method of marking that will brush off easily.

The simplest method is to use a hard lead pencil—at least a #3 lead. Soft lead leaves a darker line, but tends to smudge, leaving dirty marks on the quilt. The pencil is used with stencils, and as mentioned before, you can work directly on the top for straight-line quilting, using a ruler and pencil.

Another tool for marking straight lines is carpenter's or tailor's chalk. A carpenter's chalk line is the easiest to use, since the line is attached to a container which holds the chalk. You merely wind the line into the container to coat it with chalk, then pull it out to use. You will also need someone to help you.

Spread the quilt top out flat, either on a large table or on the floor. Position your helper on one side of the quilt while you are on the other side. Stretch the chalked line tightly across the quilt, just barely touching the surface. Lift the center of the line and snap it quickly.

Occasionally, you may want to use a design only once, as I did in the Sampler quilt. In this instance, I laid the fabric directly over the pattern and traced it through the fabric with a pencil. However, if the fabric is too heavy to see through, or colored, you can't do this. An alternative is to use dressmaker's carbon paper.

Trace the design onto a sheet of paper to make a working pattern. Position the working pattern on the block, then slip a piece of dressmaker's carbon under the pattern and trace over the design with a pencil. For a very simple design you could use a toothed tracing wheel. The tracing wheel will leave small dots rather than a solid line. The major drawback in using this method is that it may take two or three washings for the lines to come out, especially the colored carbons.

Another alternative to a stencil is the use of a transfer pencil. The transfer pencil makes an iron-on sheet that can be reused several times. It's very easy to make and it makes transferring the design a breeze. Like the dressmaker's carbon though, it may take two or three washings for the marks to come out of the fabric.

To make the transfer sheet you need only a sheet of paper and a transfer pencil. Lay the paper over the design to be transferred and trace it as you would with a regular pencil. The transfer pencil dulls quickly, so keep a pencil sharpener handy so you can maintain a fine line.

Lay the finished drawing face down on your block and press with a warm iron. I usually set it on "wool."

One other method you may want to try when quilting straight lines is the use of masking tape. With this method, you have no lines at all to remove when the quilting is finished.

Determine how far apart you want the lines to be, then buy masking tape of an appropriate width. Tear off a suitable length and press it onto the fabric in the design you have chosen. Quilt along both sides of the tape. Remove the tape and stretch a new length for your next line of quilting.

SOURCES FOR DESIGN IDEAS

No matter how many quilting designs you have available to you, the day will come when none of them quite fits the bill for the quilt you are working on. This is the time to start experimenting on your own.

Look at everyday objects in outline form, eliminating the details. This is the basis of a quilting design. When leafing through magazines look at the outline of the design, then add details as needed to suit the purpose of quilting.

Your first source of design ideas can be found among your quilting patterns. Many appliqué patterns transform beautifully into quilting designs. How about a snowflake or floral motif or the sunbonnet patterns for a child's quilt?

Examine your embroidery patterns. If you eliminate some of the details, many of them translate into quilt designs. The same is true of patterns that are intended for tole and decorative painting. And don't forget those stencil-painting patterns.

I used to recommend coloring books for simple children's designs, but after looking through some on the newsstand, I couldn't find any with simple toys and animals in outline form. If you can find some, they make great designs. You may have to add a few details to meet the requirements of quilting. As an alternative, look for pictures that you can simplify for quilting.

Many patterns designed for other crafts can be made into quilting designs. I recently saw a basket pattern designed for cut-paper silhouettes that would make a beautiful quilting design. One design in this book was taken directly from the wallpaper in my bathroom.

When all else fails you can always fall back on folded paper cutouts. Cut a sheet of paper the size of the desired block design, then fold it two, three or four times, lengthwise, crosswise, on the diagonal. Now cut designs along the folds. Open it out to see what you have created. If you don't like it, try again.

Quilting

Now that you have selected a design and marked the top, you are almost ready to start the actual quilting. Before we get into that though, we should discuss a few of the additional supplies you will need.

BATTS/FILLERS

In the past, many materials were used for the filler in the quilt. Commercial batts weren't always available and the ladies used what was handy. Some old quilts were filled with straw or cornhusks and even paper has been used. Fleece from sheared sheep was often used, and the adage "waste not, want not" prompted the use of old wool or flannel blankets for the filler.

While blankets are still not a bad choice, the modern quilter has a variety of batts to choose from, depending on the effect desired and the personal preferences of the quilter.

Cotton Batts. Long-time quilters will be familiar with the cotton batt because at one time this was the only commercial batt available. The characteristics of the cotton batt were what dictated the extremely close quilting of yesteryear. With wear and washing, cotton tends to lump up and shift if it is not well anchored by quilting. Many quilters prefer the cotton batt for the same reasons they choose cotton fabric for the top; it is easy to sew through. Many also prefer the flat, thin appearance of the finished quilt because it best duplicates the look of an old quilt.

Polyester Batts. This is a synthetic material that is easy to work with. It comes in a wide range of weights ranging from those duplicating the thin look of cotton to high-loft weights that give a thick puffy look to the finished quilt.

Bonded batts have been treated with chemicals to ensure that they will not shred or tear, thereby giving a smooth uniform surface. The batt feels rather stiff, but the finished quilt has a higher loft than a cotton batt so that the quilting stitches stand out in higher relief. It does not need to be quilted as closely as the cotton batt, which allows greater flexibility in choice of design and lends itself beautifully to special effects. Quilting lines can be anywhere from two to four inches apart.

Unbonded Batts. These batts are untreated so that they remain soft and fluffy. They have the same ease in sewing and high loft as the bonded batts, but care must be taken when spreading the batt since it will shred, leaving thick and thin spots. You will have to pull off pieces from the thick spots or along the edges to fill in the thin areas. This batt, however, gives a softer look than the bonded batt, and once quilted will not shift. The quilting can be spaced two to four inches apart.

For hand quilting, you will also need a frame. If you have the space you can use a full-sized frame which allows you to stretch the whole quilt before you begin sewing. If space is a problem, a quilting hoop will serve equally well, although you have to keep moving the quilt as you complete each section.

To prepare the quilt for mounting, you must first assemble the three layers of the quilt: the backing, the filler or batt, and the top. Spread the backing out flat on the floor, then spread the batt over the backing, stretching slightly to fit, if necessary. Now lay the pressed top on the batt and smooth it out. Baste the three layers together diagonally, horizontally and vertically. The quilt is now ready to mount.

With the quilt stretched out on the floor, lay one of the muslin-covered bars of the frame at the top of the quilt and the other bar at the bottom. Using heavy thread, baste the quilt to the bars, making sure it is secured tightly enough to withstand the stretching action of the frame.

Roll the quilt tightly onto one bar, leaving enough free to stretch across the frame. Replace the bars in the frame, adjusting the quilt so that it is stretched tautly in the frame.

If using a hoop, follow the same procedure for basting. Place the quilt in the hoop, starting in the center and working towards the edges. Quilt this center section, then move the hoop outward for the next section. When that section is complete, move the hoop to one side or the other of the center section so that the top is worked evenly from the center to the edges. When you reach the edges, you may have to dispense with the hoop and quilt the remainder in your lap.

The Quilting Stitch. The quilting stitch is a very fine running stitch worked with a short needle and quilting thread. It is difficult to get the hang of taking several stitches on the needle before pulling the thread through, but with practice, you can master the technique.

Make a small knot in the end of the thread and pull it through from the back. Give a sharp tug on the thread to pull the knot through the backing fabric into the batting. Hold the material down with your other hand and push the needle straight down and bring the tip up near the point of entry. Take three or four stitches in this manner, then pull the needle all the way through the fabric and repeat.

If you find it too difficult to master this method of quilting, you might want to try the stab stitch. It is slower than the running stitch, but the results are the same. Start the thread in the same way as before. Place your left hand (or right hand if you are left-handed) on the underside of the quilt. Push the needle straight down through the three layers and catch it with your other hand. Push the needle straight up a short distance away. Take small evenly spaced stitches aiming for ten to fifteen stitches to the inch.

You will also need a thimble or finger guard to protect your fingers from the pricks of the needle.

Machine Quilting. I am a firm believer in machine quilting. In fact, my hand quilting is so bad and takes so long, that I've given it up entirely and do all my quilting on the machine. And contrary to popular opinion, any design can be machine quilted as in the Sampler quilt.

If you have ever done machine embroidery, you'll have no problems with machine quilting, and even if you haven't it won't take long to get the knack of manipulating the quilt under the needle.

First, a word of warning. If you are planning to enter your quilts in competition, check the rules before you machine quilt. Many shows insist that the quilting be done by hand.

You are also going to discover that my methods differ drastically from those of other writers, but do try them before you decide that this is not the proper way to do things.

My main divergence from the "norm" is that I do not baste the three layers together before sewing. The outstanding characteristic of fabric is that it does stretch, so rather than trying to bludgeon it into submission with extensive basting, I make allowances for this characteristic.

Step one is to loosen the pressure on the presser foot. Either set the machine for darn or remove the pressure altogether. Some instructions I've read say that after you have basted thoroughly, tighten the pressure on the presser foot. However, this causes the foot to grab the fabric, causing puckers that pile up on the basting lines. Even normal pressure will cause the stitches to pile up on the basting lines.

Since I am not going to baste the layers together, my second step must be to assume that I will have some shifting of the fabric. To make allowance for this, I cut the backing fabric one or two inches larger all around, depending on whether I am quilting the whole top or by the block. A bit more shifting can be expected if you are quilting the whole top. Lay the backing out on the floor and smooth it out. Spread the batting over the backing, making sure it reaches the edges. Now spread the top over the batting and pin it with straight pins here and there. I've actually found very little slippage in the three layers since the cloth seems to stick to the batting.

If you are quilting the whole top as a unit, it is easier if you use outline quilting or straight-line quilting. The quilt is quite heavy and not very maneuverable. A large table on which to sew is an absolute must. It helps keep the quilt flat, thus cutting down on any shifting. Position your machine at one end of the table so you can spread the quilt out and support the weight of it.

Slide the edge of the quilt under the presser foot and roll it up to the center. The center section is the most difficult because so much fabric is rolled under the machine. As you move out towards the edges it gets easier. Following the seam line from the center, stitch to the outer edge of the quilt, smoothing out the fabric as you go. Stitch two or three rows in this direction, then turn the quilt and stitch two or three rows in the opposite direction. Check frequently to make sure that the backing fabric is still smooth. This alternating technique helps keep the quilt smooth and flat.

If your top is of a simple design that requires only straight-line stitching, you can start at one end of the quilt and work to the other end. In this case, the backing fabric should be longer on the end and sides towards which you are sewing so that any shift in the fabric is covered by the backing when finished. Always start sewing from the same end.

If you are quilting an intricate design it is easier to quilt by the block or in sections of four or six blocks. You can also do it in strips of blocks.

When quilting by the block or in small sections, there will be less shifting of the fabric so that the backing can be cut only one inch larger all around than the block or strips. Cut the batting the size of the quilt top section or block. Quilt in the design being sure not to quilt beyond the seam line into the seam allowance.

To assemble the quilted blocks, trim the backing even with the quilt block. Lay the quilted blocks right sides together, matching seams and pin, being sure to fold the backing out of the way so that it doesn't catch in the seam line. Stitch the blocks together, adding blocks in the same manner to complete the first row. Before adding the next row or section I've found it easier to finish the seams on the back. Turn the quilt over and smooth it out. Smooth one edge of the backing over the seam line, and under the other edge being sure that the quilt top remains flat. Fold under the seam allowance on the other edge and lay it over the first edge. Stitch in place with a slipstitch. Now go back and finish the quilting across the seams. The seams on the back will fade into the quilting.

If you have quilted by the block and find the seams on the back objectionable, a nice finish is to lay lattice strips over the seams. This forms a nice frame around each block on the back of the quilt.

INSTRUCTIONS FOR SAMPLER QUILT:

QUILT SIZE: 74″ × 88″

Pieces Needed for Quilt

A	Red	180
	Blue	259
B	Red	518
	Blue	360

Center Squares   Thirty 11″ squares, finished size 10″

FABRIC REQUIREMENTS 45″ fabric

White	4⅓ yards
Red	5¼ yards
Blue	5⅔ yards

Directions for Piecing

Flying Geese design with red center triangle flanked by blue: Piece 180 red A to 360 blue B. Assemble these into strips of five. You will need thirty-six strips.

Flying Geese design with blue center triangle flanked by red: Piece 259 blue A to 518 red B. Assemble these completed units into strips thirty-seven units long. You need seven such strips.

Cut out thirty 11″ white blocks. This allows for a one-half-inch seam allowance. Beginning in the upper-left corner, seam a five-unit strip to a white block, with the geese pointing to the top of the block. Add another five-unit strip to the other side of the block with the geese going downwards. Add four more white blocks with alternate Flying Geese strips, alternating the direction of the geese with each block. The final strip will be pointing down. Sew a thirty-seven-unit strip to the top and bottom of the first row with the top strip going to the left and the bottom one going to the right.

The preceding instructions are the traditional way of piecing the strips, and the quilting is done when the whole top has been joined. I used the sewing machine to piece and quilt the entire top.

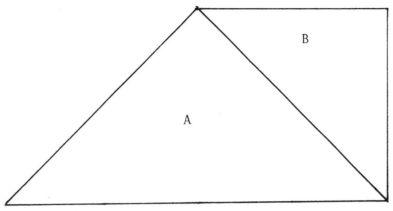

Illus. 15. Flying Geese pattern.

I have had difficulty matching the seams for A and B when using the traditional method so I made each Flying Geese into two squares made up of half-triangles, then used a speed-sewing method of sewing them.

In this method, you mark the fabric directly rather than using a template. On a large table spread out your blue fabric, face up. Lay the red fabric on top of the blue with the right side of the red down. The wrong sides of both fabrics are facing out, with right sides together.

I then cut out a long plastic template measuring three and three-fourths inches wide. Pin the two lengths of fabric together and draw a straight line across the width of the red fabric. Lay the template edge on this line and draw along it, moving it, if necessary, to mark the entire width. Move the template down and mark the next row. After you have several rows marked crosswise, lay the template lengthwise and mark, crossing the crosswise lines to form squares. You will need a total of 439 squares since each square makes two units.

Mark each square diagonally in one direction only. Measure one-half inch on each side of this diagonal line and mark again. This is a breeze if you have a plastic see-through ruler. Your fabric should look like Illus. 17.

Sew along the dashed lines, but do not sew

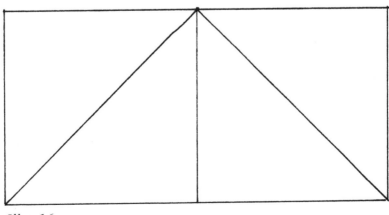

Illus 16.

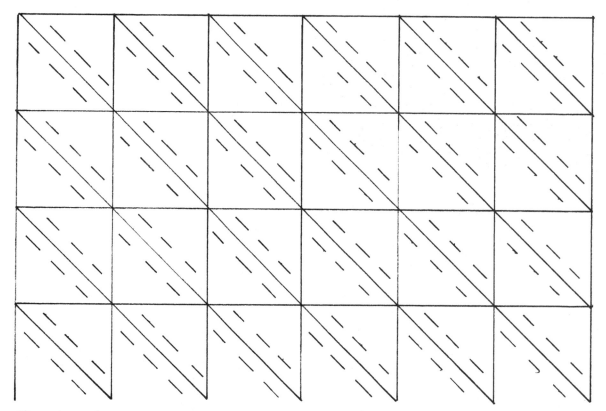

Illus. 17. 3¾" squares. The dashed line is the sewing line and the solid line is the cutting line.

across the solid line. Lift the presser foot and move the fabric to the end of the next dashed line. There is no need to cut the thread. When the sewing is completed, cut along the solid lines. You now have a perfect square with one half red and the other half blue. Press all seams to one side. As you press them, stack the units in four matched piles, two piles with the red forming the center triangle and two piles with the blue forming the triangle. You will need 180 red triangle units, and 259 blue triangle units.

Go back to the machine and sew these units together as you have them laid out, using an assembly-line system, just feeding them through the machine one after the other. Clip the units apart and press.

At this point, set aside the blue triangle units and join the red triangle units into thirty-six strips of five. Press the seams in one direction.

I assembled and quilted the quilt in sections; three sections made up of four blocks and their adjoining strips and three sections of six blocks with their strips set in two rows.

I marked all the center blocks with their quilting designs before setting them together, so that I could space them in a pleasing manner throughout the quilt.

Again, starting in the upper-left-hand corner, sew one of the five-unit strips to the outside edge of the block, with the triangles going upwards. Add the next strip to the opposite side of the block with the triangles going down. Add another block to this strip then one more strip with the triangles going up. Make two identical rows.

Using the units you set aside, make three strips sixteen units long. Sew one strip to the top of the two-block row, having the triangles going towards the left. Sew the next strip to the bottom of the row, with the triangles going to the right. Add the next row and the last strip facing to the left. Quilt this section.

To finish the two top rows, the next section will consist of two rows of three blocks and strips. The direction of the strips will continue in the pattern established by the first section. Since you already have a strip unit on the first four-block section, you start this section with a plain block, then a strip, then a block, and so forth. See Illus. 18 for the assembly diagram for the quilt top.

The Flying Geese strips were outline quilted following the appearance of the design rather than the actual seams. On the edges where the seams join, I quilted only half of the strip, leaving the other half free to make it easier to sew the sections together. I then went back and quilted over the areas left free to form a continuous quilting line on the back of the quilt.

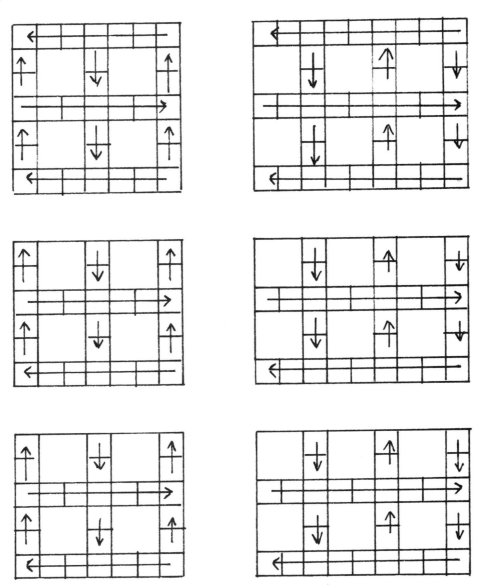

Illus. 18. Assembly diagram, showing direction of Flying Geese strips.

FEATHER BLOCKS

Illus. 19.

21

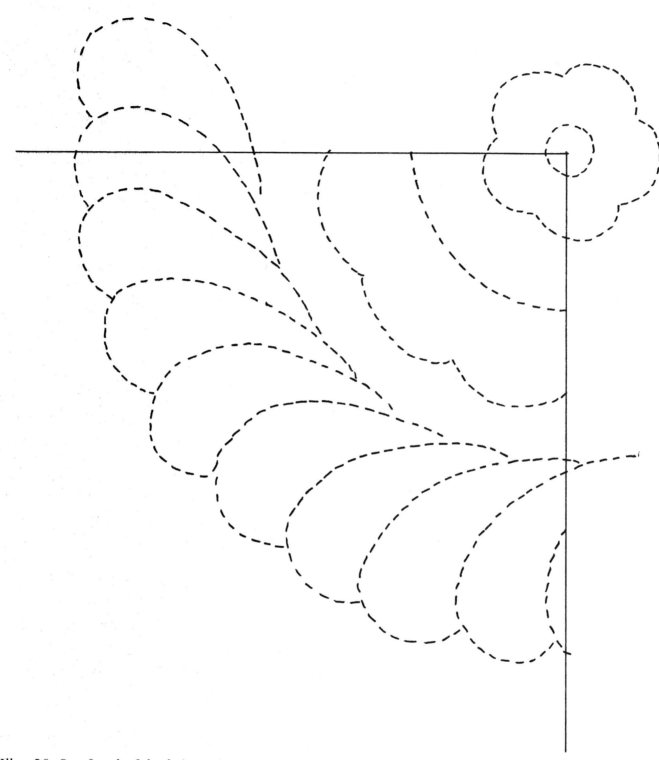

Illus. 20. One fourth of the design.

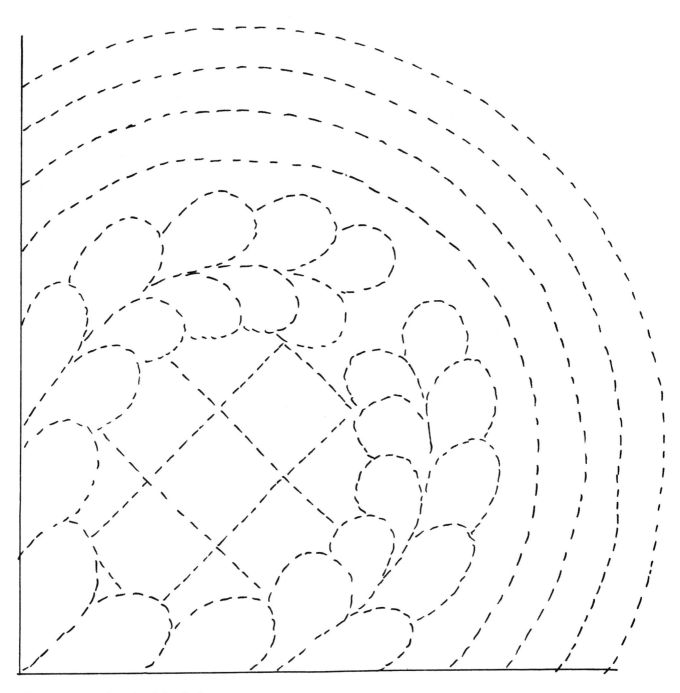

Illus. 21. One fourth of the design.

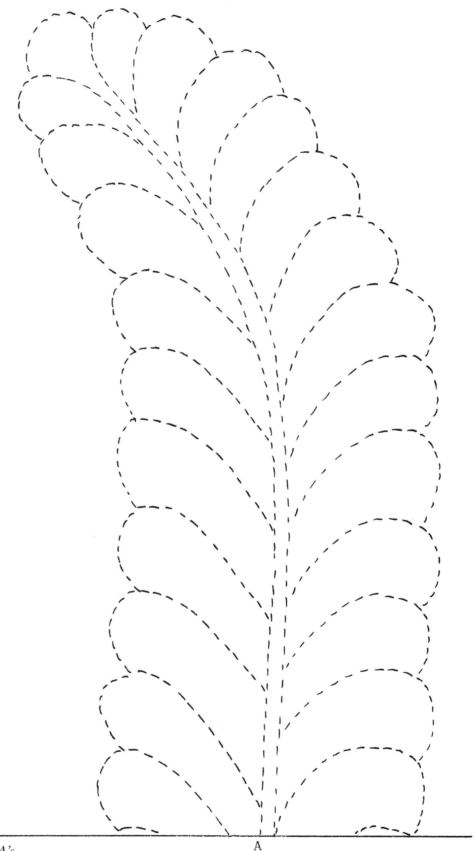

Illus. 22. Match A's.

A

24

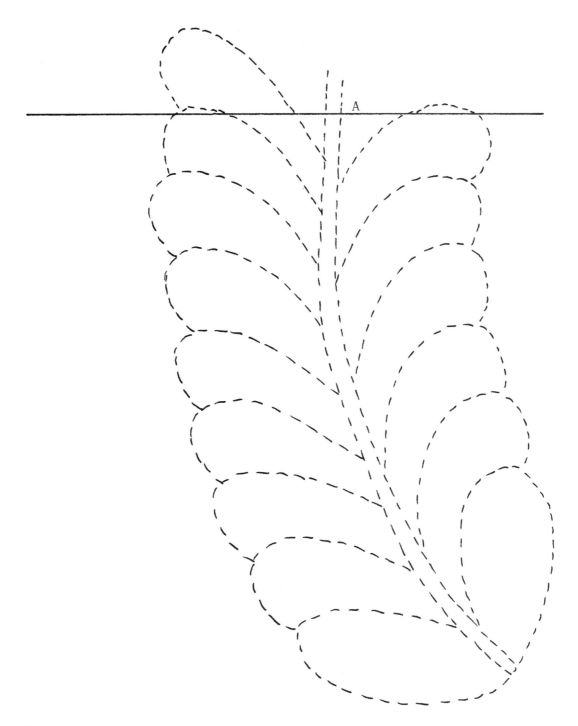

Illus. 22 (continued). Match A's.

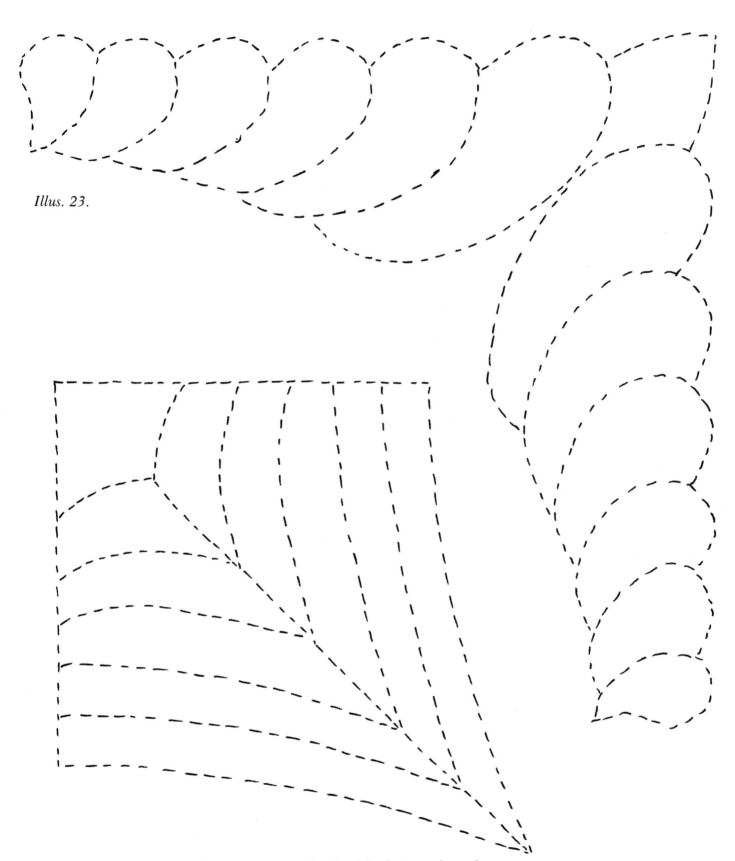

Illus. 23.

Illus. 24. Make the square edges represent one fourth of the design or have the pointed edges meet in the middle, repeating two times for half a design, or four times for a square one.

Illus. 25.

Illus. 26. This is the original design. See the following pages for variations based on this.

28

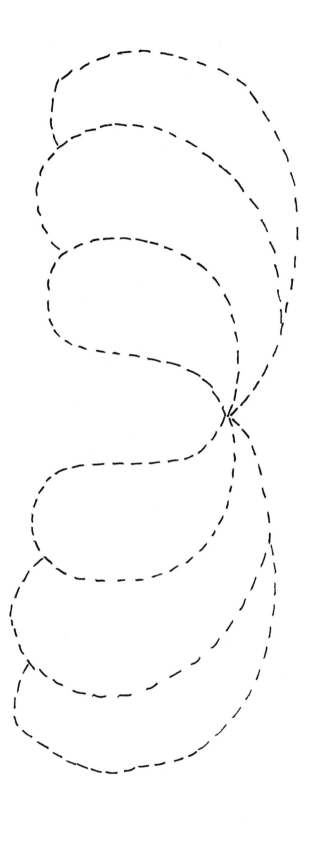

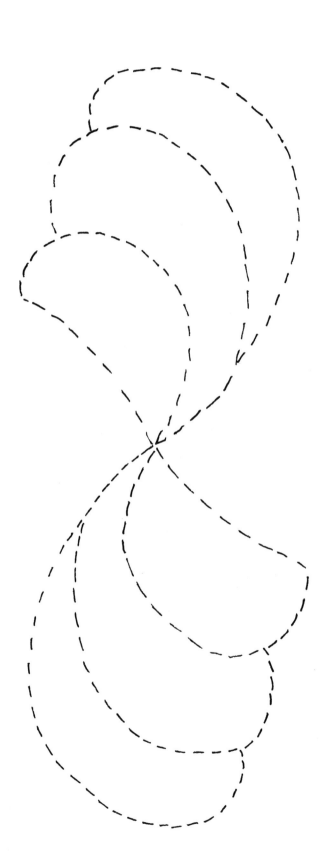

Illus. 27. Variations using the feather portion of the preceding design.

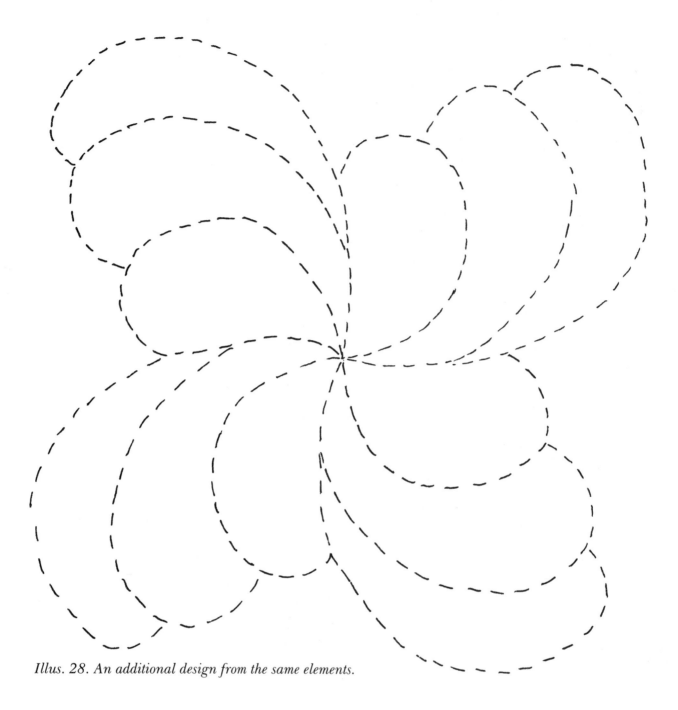

Illus. 28. An additional design from the same elements.

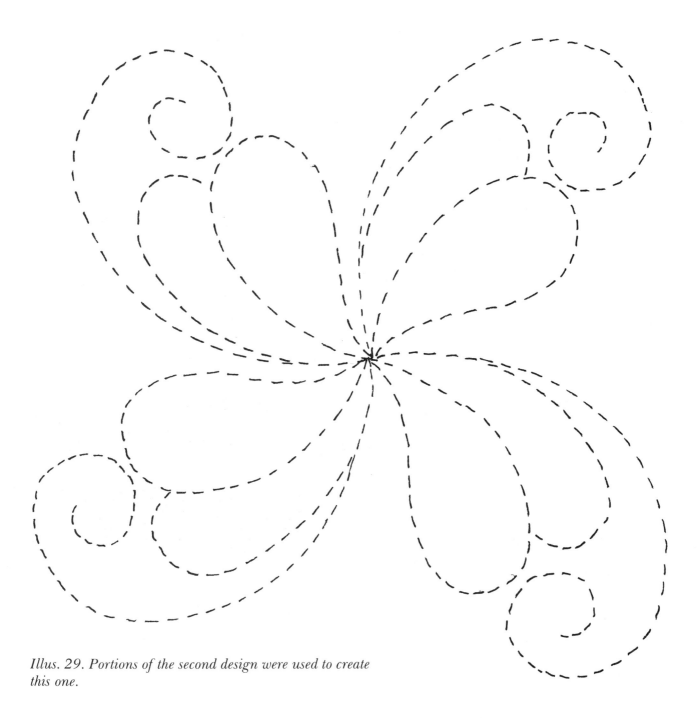

Illus. 29. Portions of the second design were used to create this one.

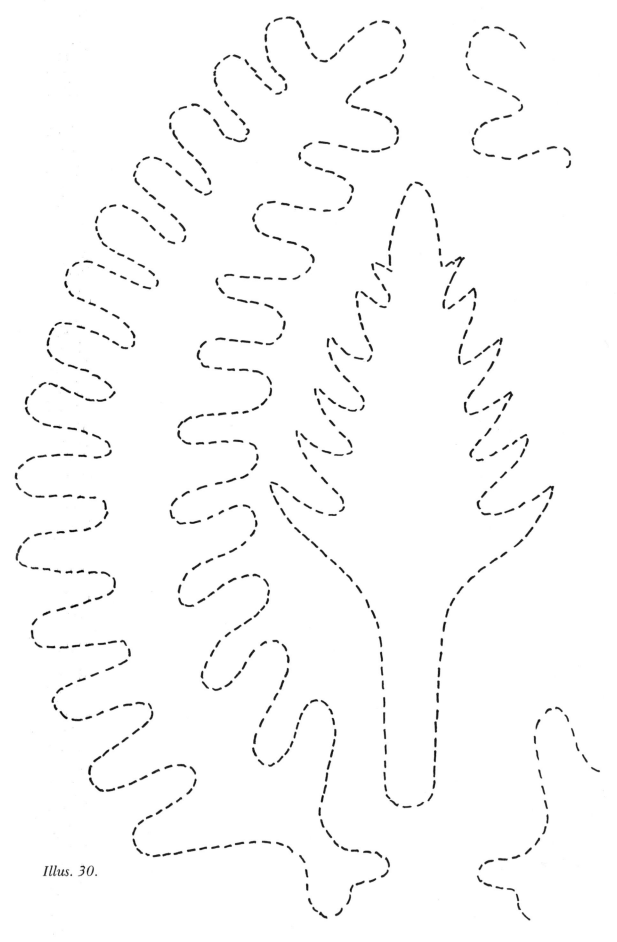

Illus. 30.

Illus. 31. Match letters, Illus. 32.

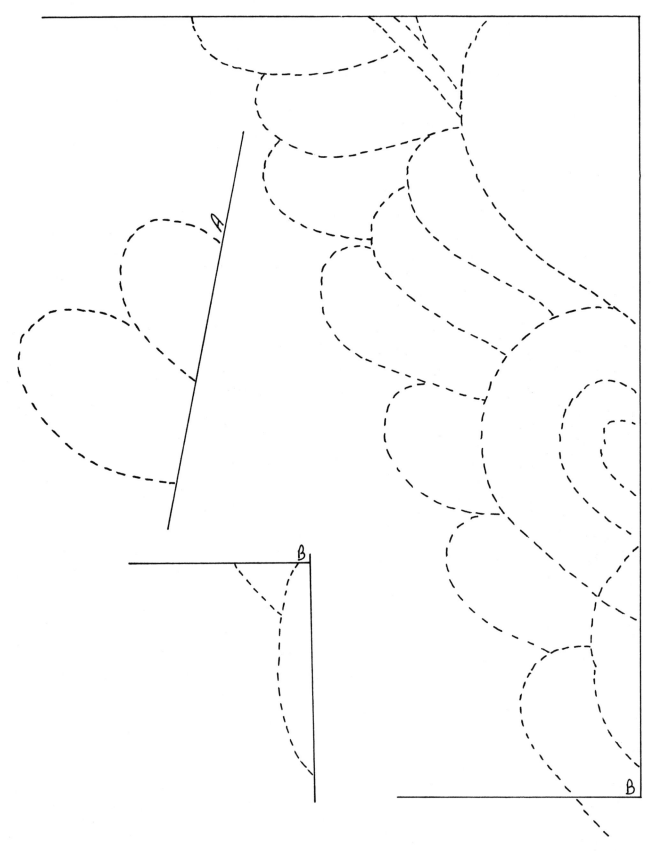

Illus. 32. Match letters.

Illus. 33. One fourth of the design.

Illus. 34. One half of the design.

Illus. 35. One half of the design.

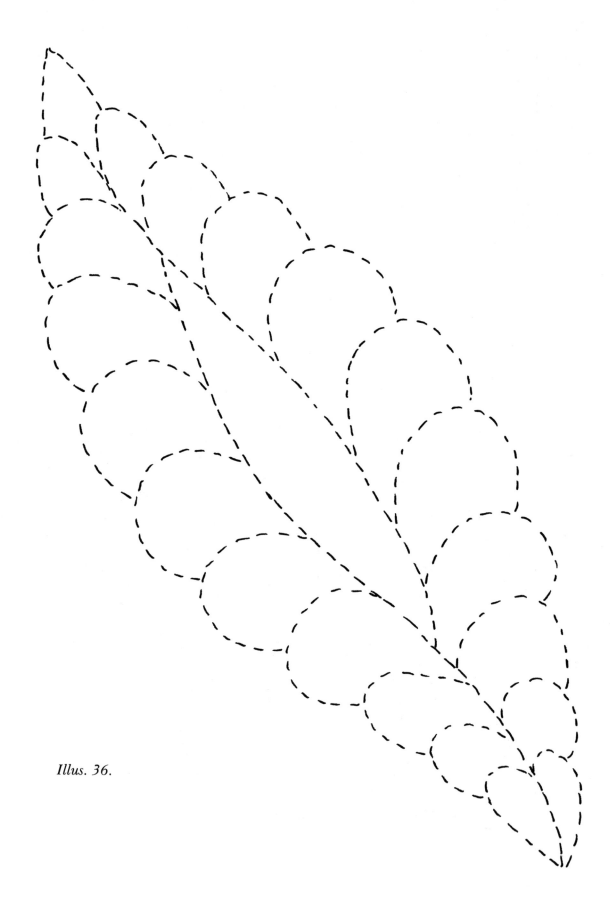

Illus. 36.

Illus. 37.

SMALL DESIGNS AND MISCELLANEOUS

Illus. 38.

Illus. 39.

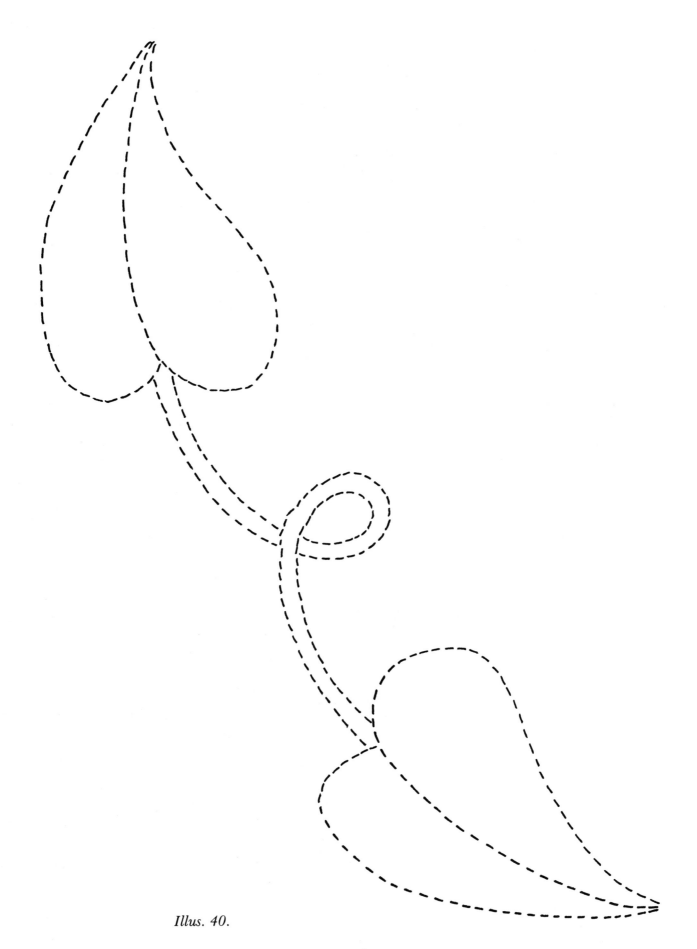

Illus. 40.

43

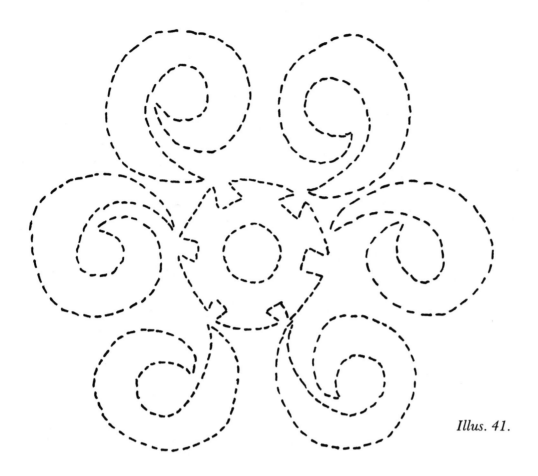

Illus. 41.

Illus. 42.

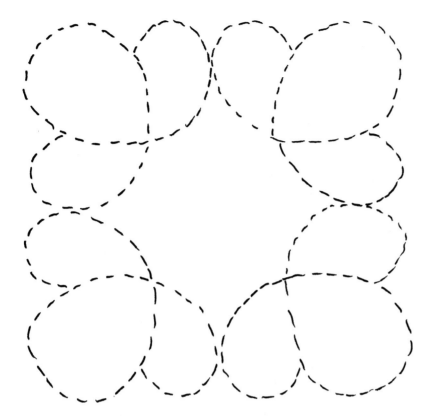

Illus. 43.

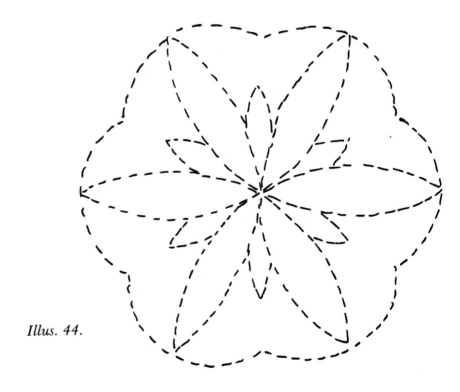

Illus. 44.

45

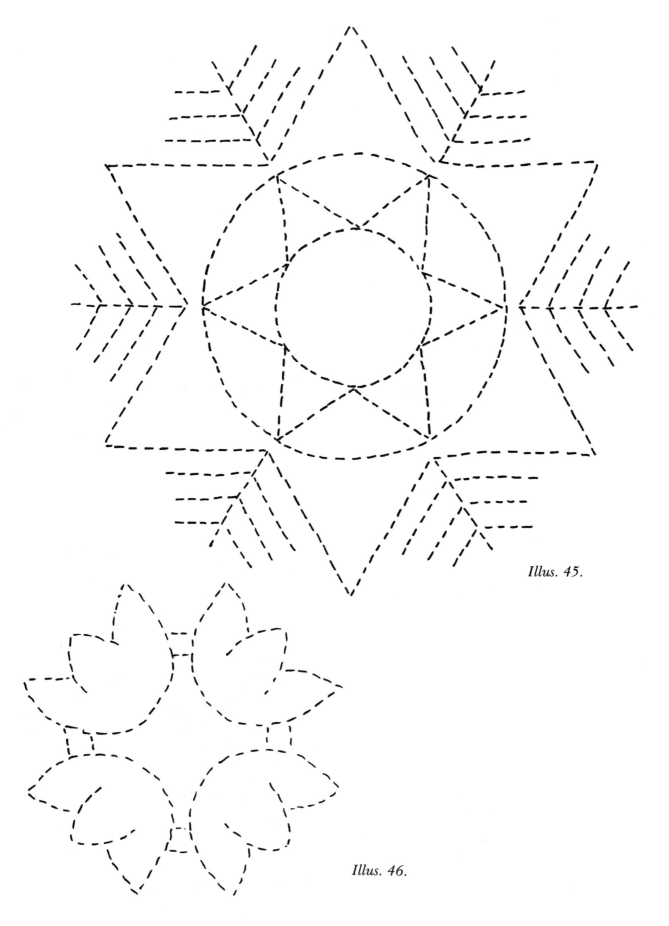

Illus. 45.

Illus. 46.

46

Illus. 47.

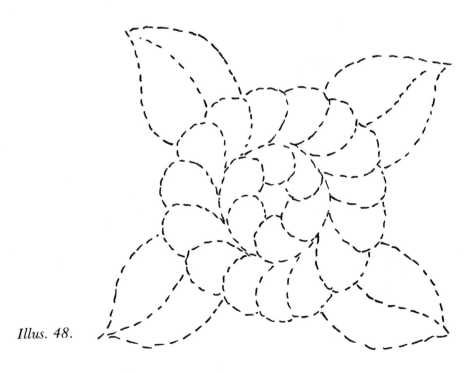

Illus. 48.

47

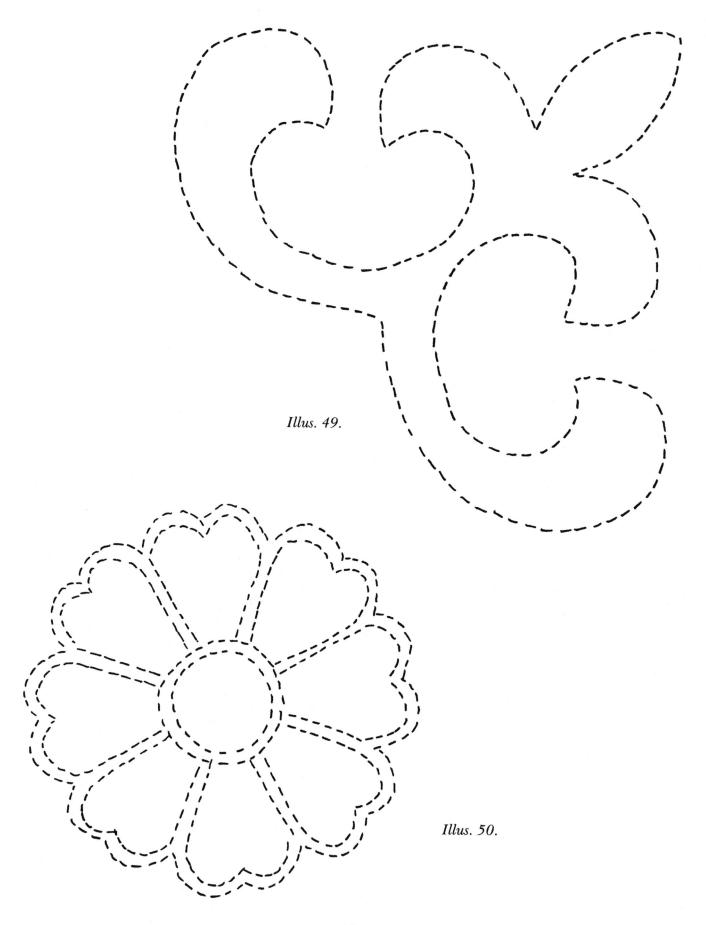

Illus. 49.

Illus. 50.

48

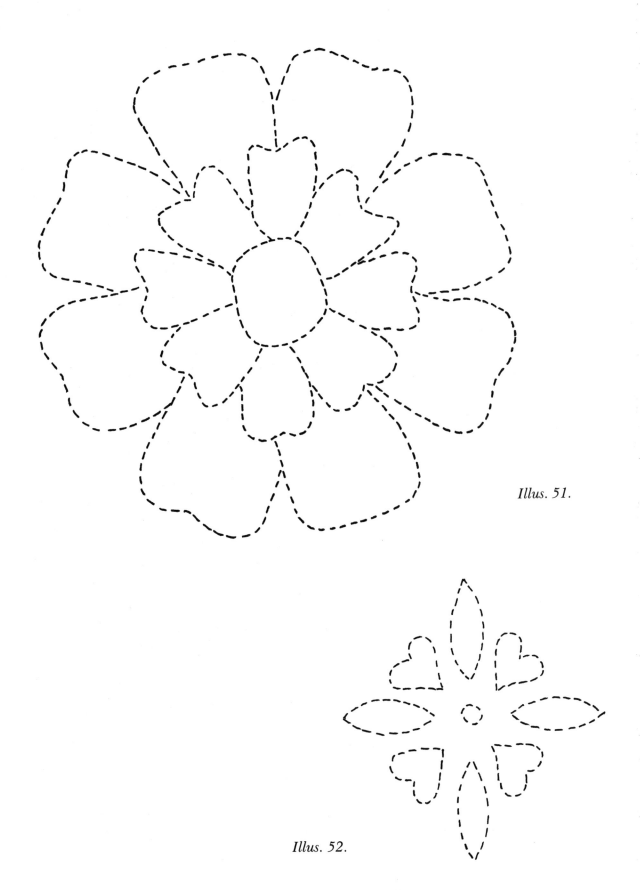

Illus. 51.

Illus. 52.

49

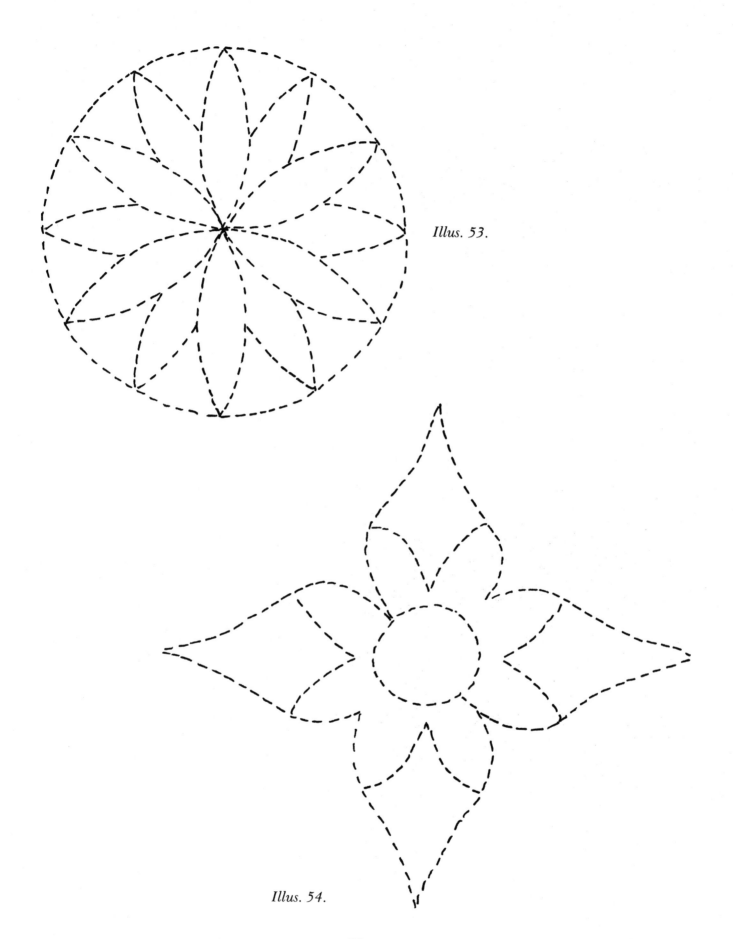

Illus. 53.

Illus. 54.

50

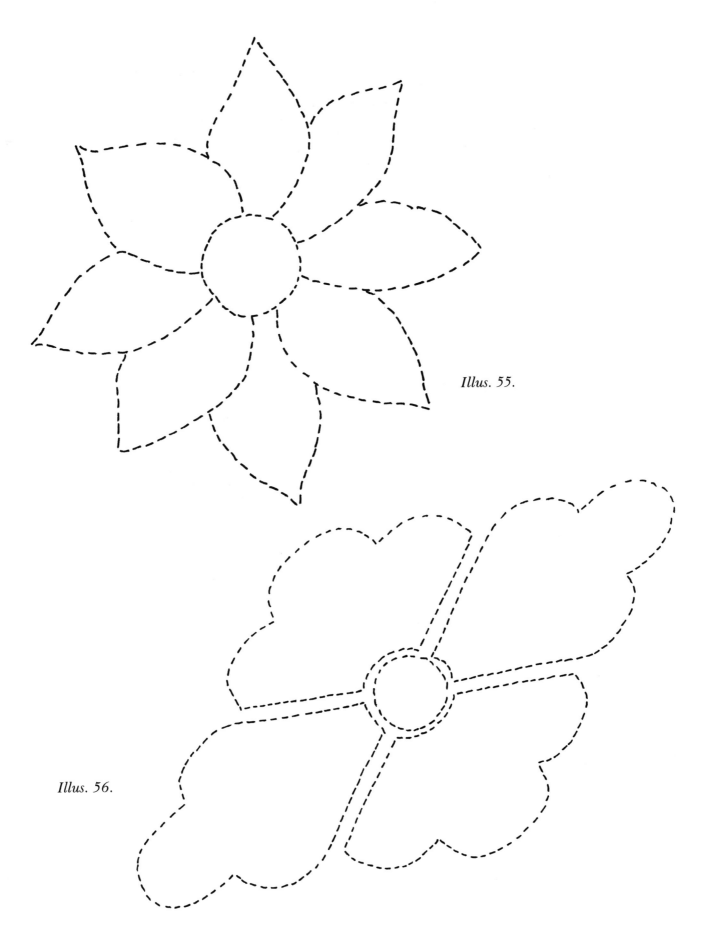

Illus. 55.

Illus. 56.

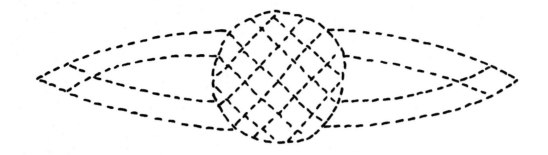

Illus. 57.

Illus. 58.

BLOCK DESIGNS

Illus. 59

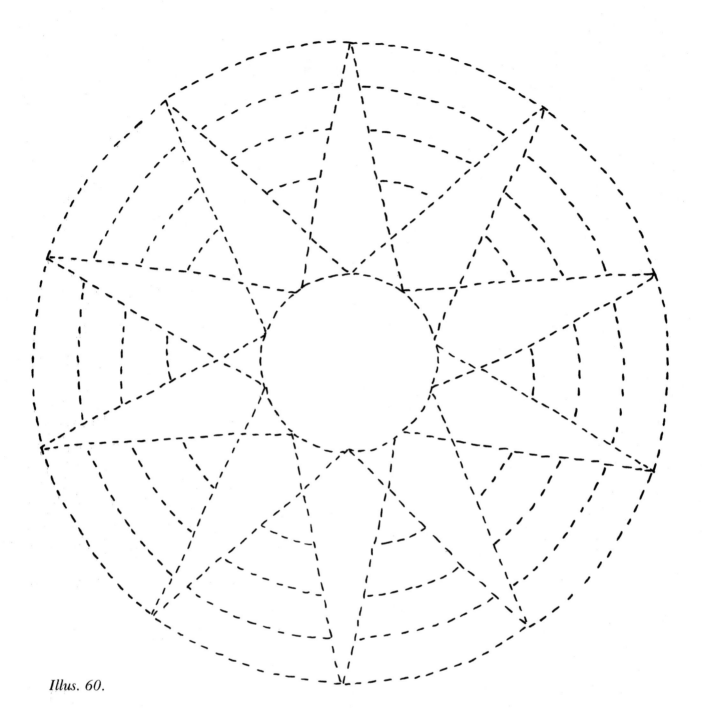

Illus. 60.

Illus. 61.

Illus. 62.

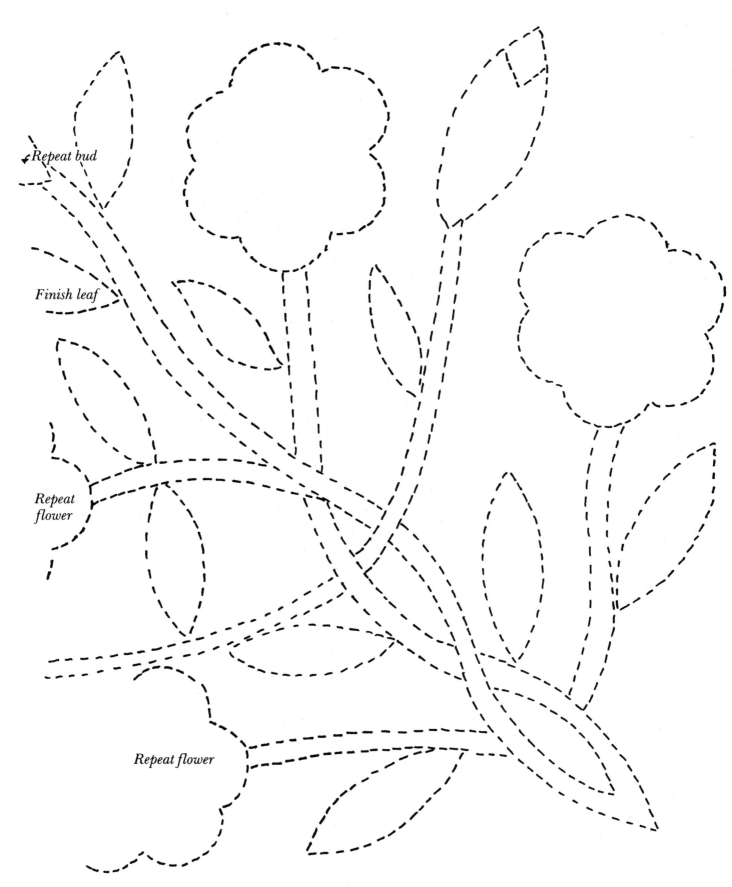

Repeat bud

Finish leaf

Repeat
flower

Repeat flower

Illus. 63.

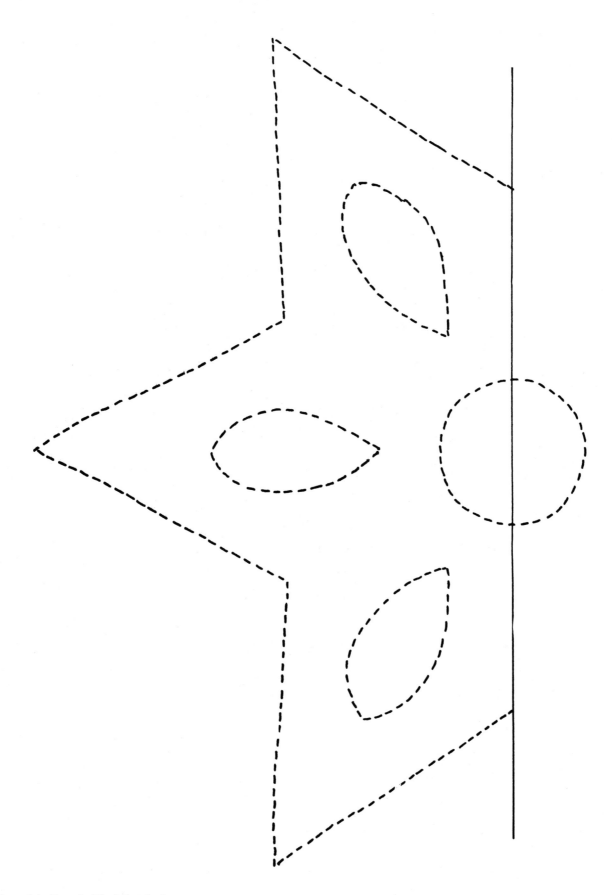

Illus. 64. One half of the design.

Illus. 65. One half of the design.

Illus. 66. One fourth of the design.

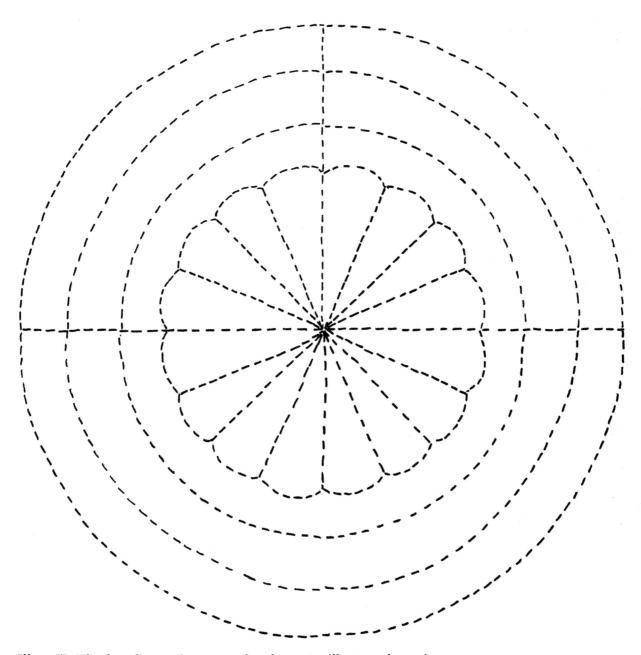

Illus. 67. The three lines going out to the edge are to illustrate the various ways this design can be used.

61

Illus. 68.

Illus. 69.

63

Illus. 70.

Illus. 71. For complete pattern, reverse your pattern sheet and line up the small circle at base.

65

Illus. 72.

Illus. 73.

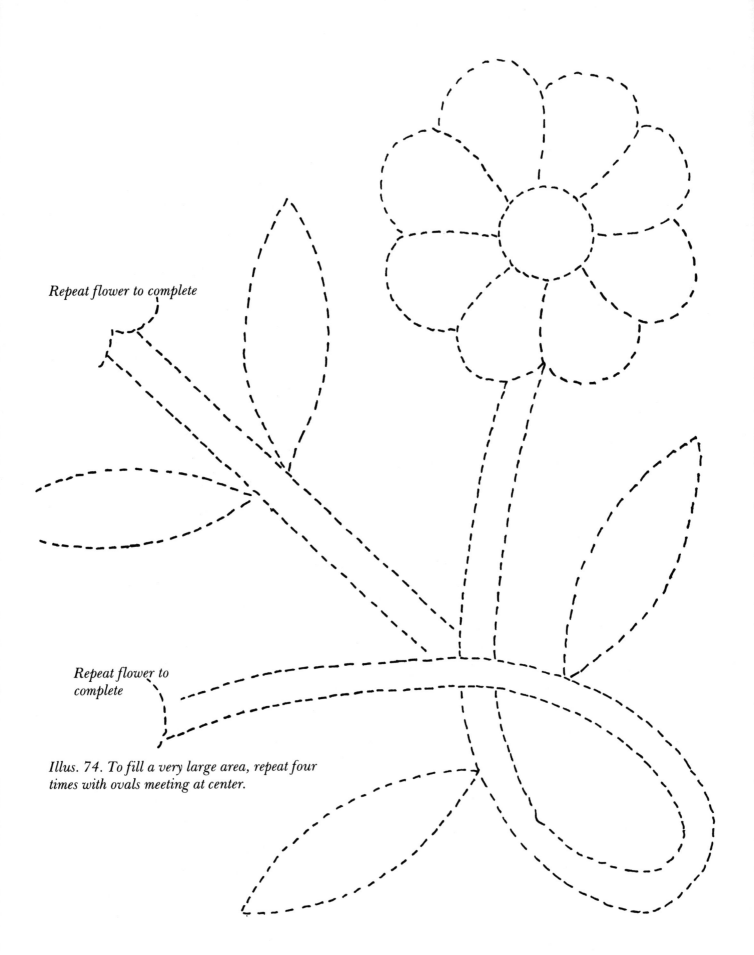

Repeat flower to complete

Repeat flower to complete

Illus. 74. To fill a very large area, repeat four times with ovals meeting at center.

68

Illus. 75.

Illus. 76. Use either singly or match bottom of leaf at center for large areas.

70

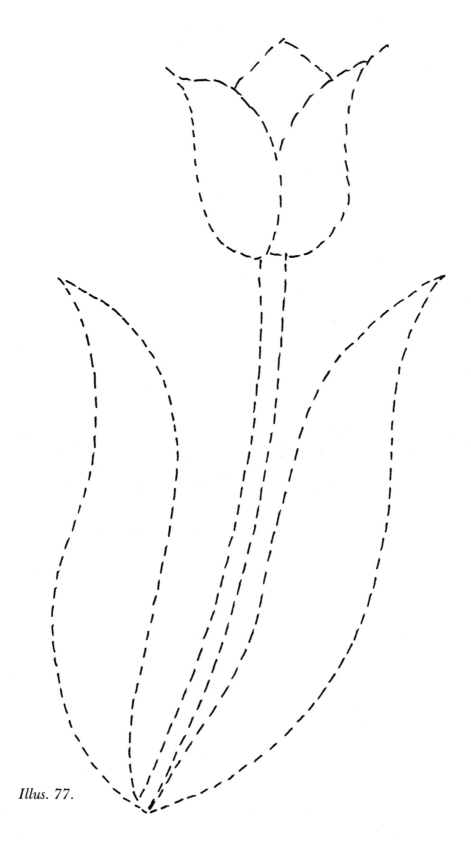

Illus. 77.

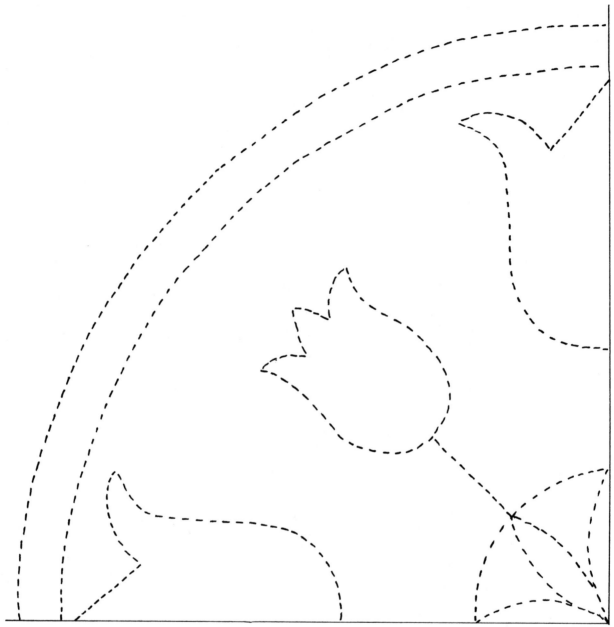

Illus. 78. One fourth of the design.

Illus. 79. One half of the design.

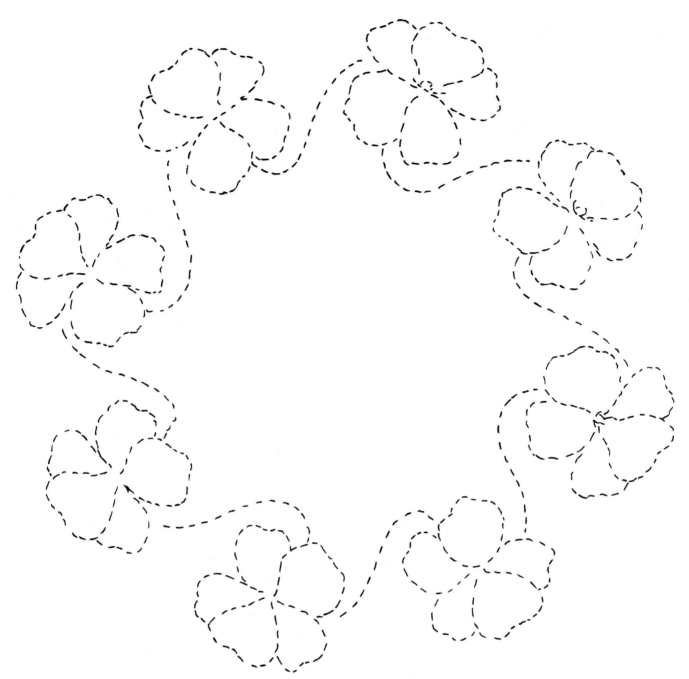

Illus. 80.

Illus. 81.

Illus. 82.

Illus. 83.

Illus. 84.

Illus. 85.

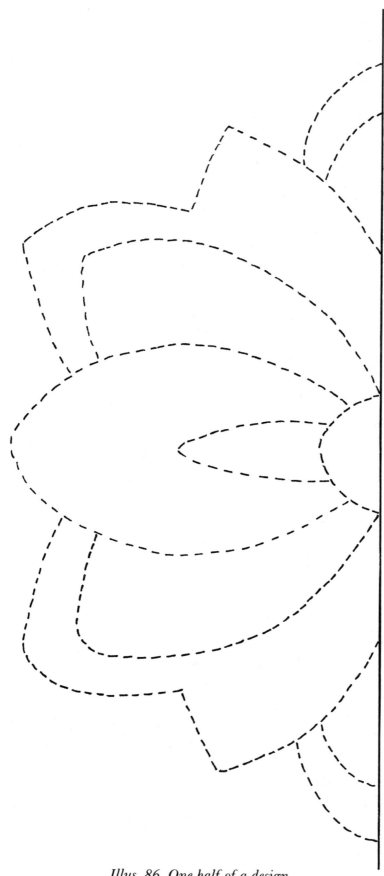

Illus. 86. One half of a design.

Illus. 87.

Illus. 88.

Illus. 89.

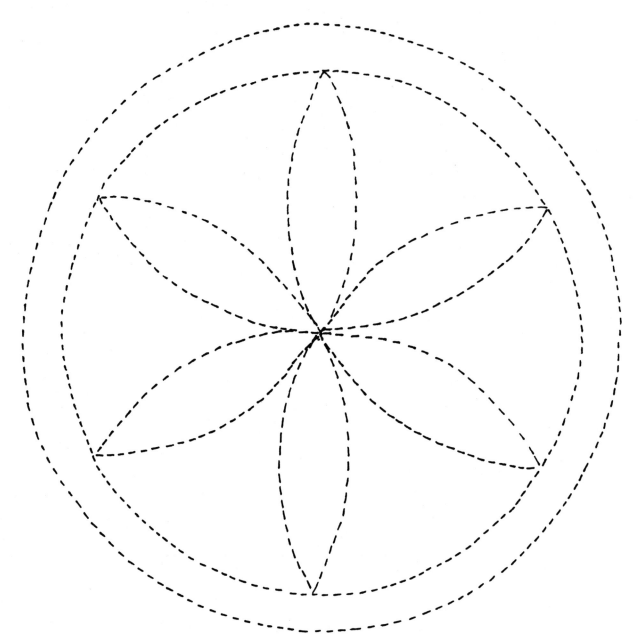

Illus. 90.

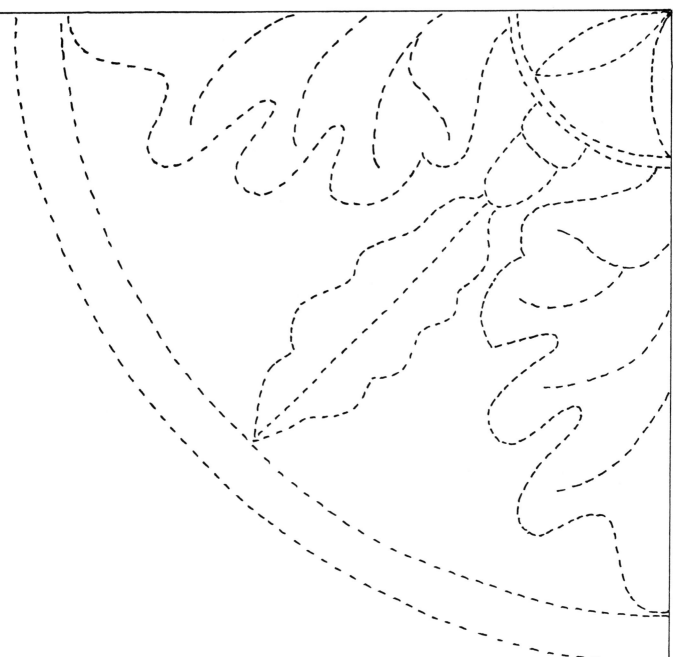

Illus. 91. One fourth of a design.

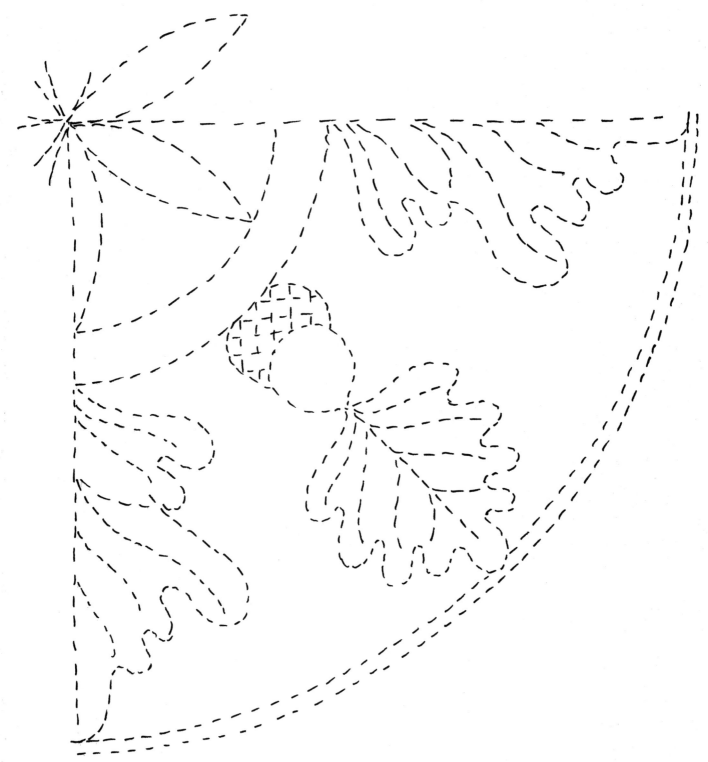

Illus. 92. One fourth of a design.

Illus. 93.

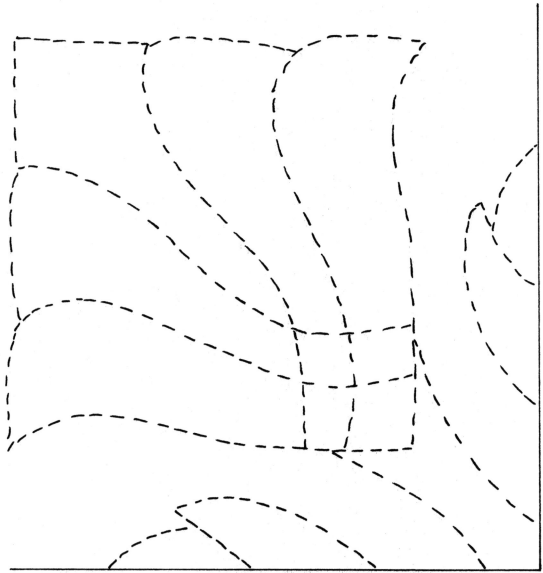

Illus. 94. One fourth of a design.

Illus. 95.

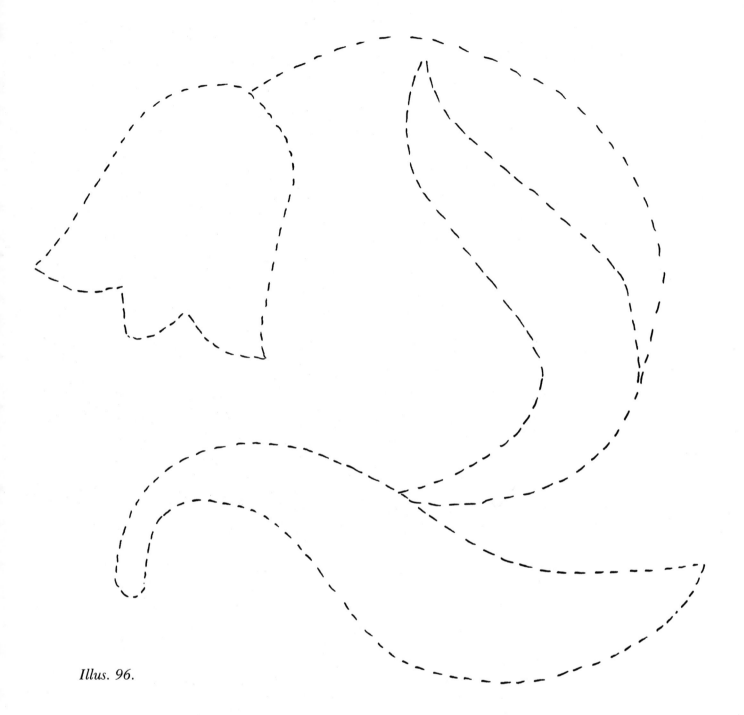

Illus. 96.

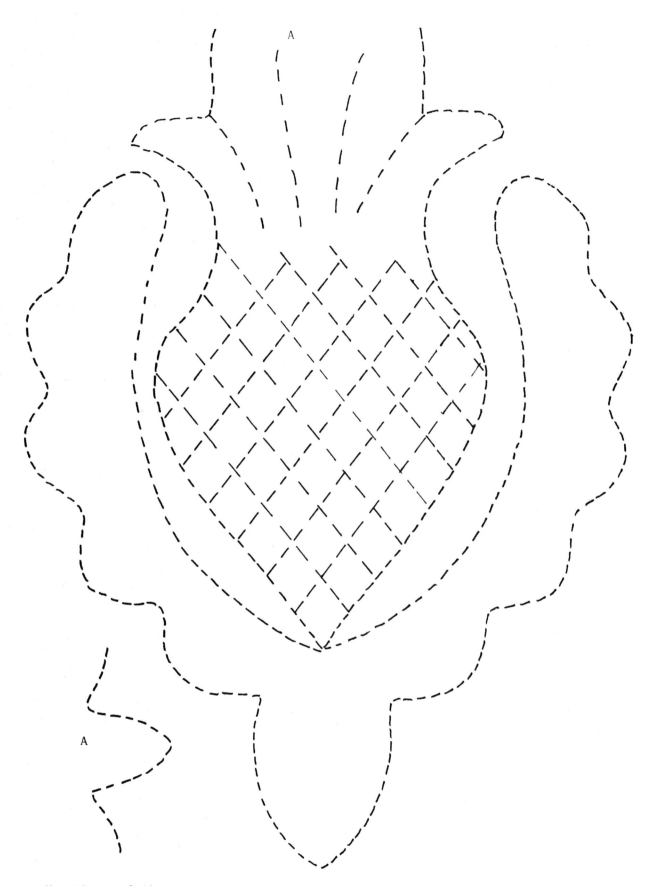

Illus. 97. Match A's.

Illus. 98.

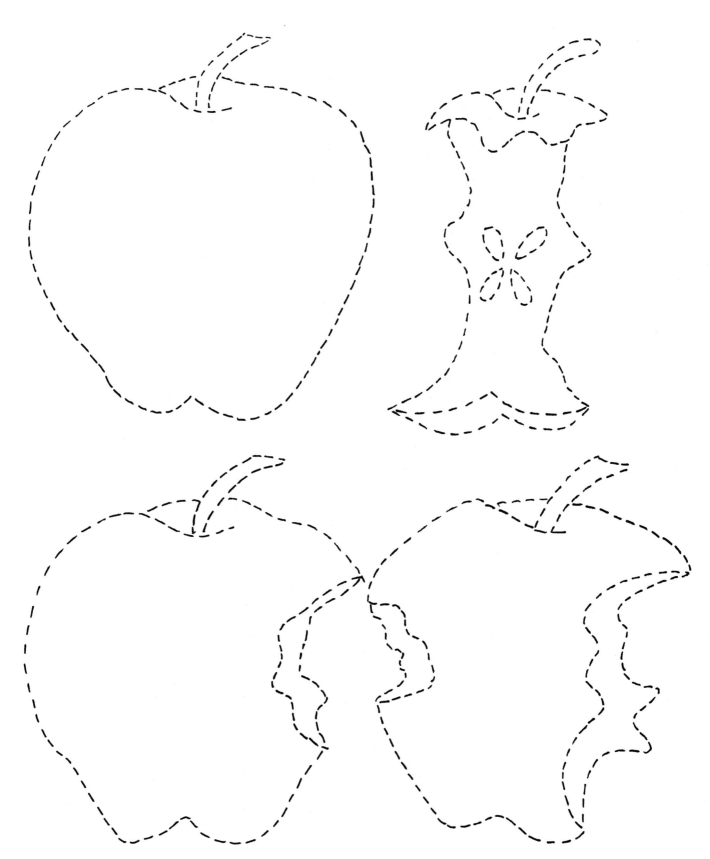

Illus. 99. For a touch of whimsy.

Illus. 100. To complete design reverse the pattern and match at X.

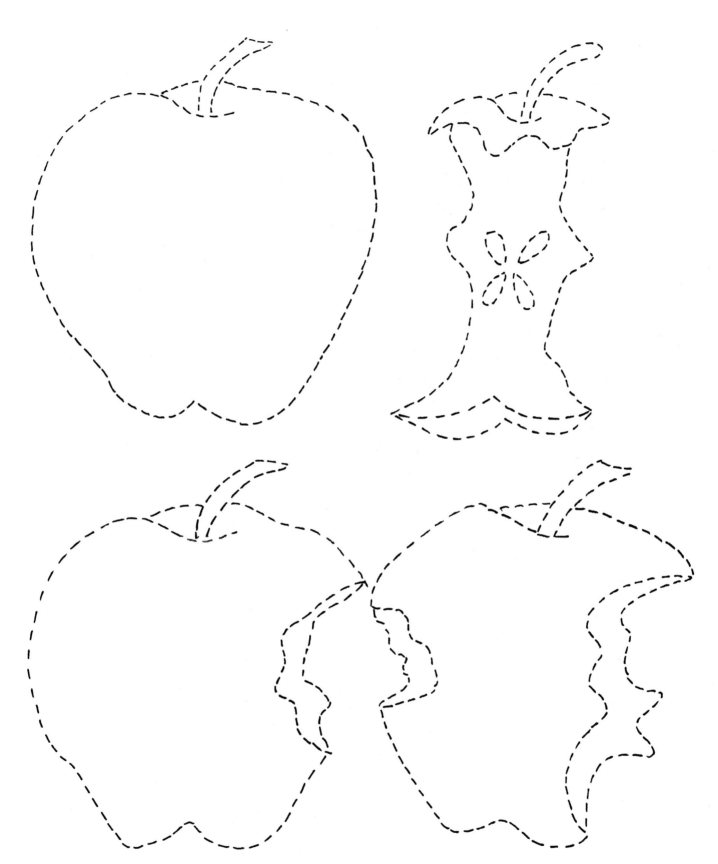

Illus. 99. For a touch of whimsy.

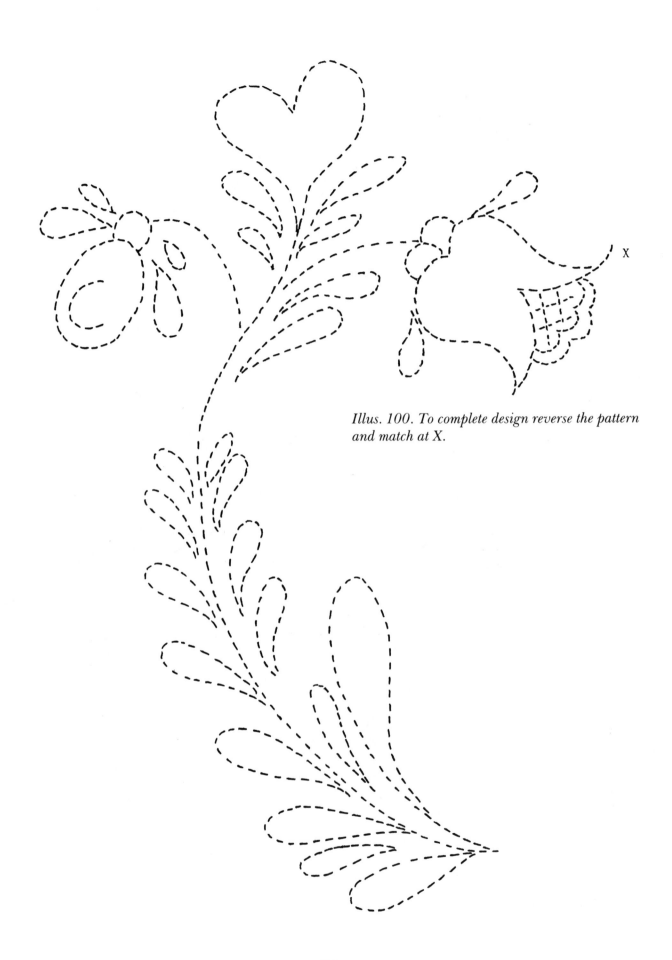

Illus. 100. To complete design reverse the pattern and match at X.

Illus. 101. Turn the design over and trace it going in the opposite direction to provide a curvy border.

Illus. 102.

BUTTERFLIES
AND EAGLES

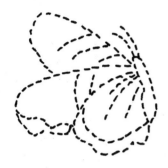

Illus. 103.

Illus. 104.

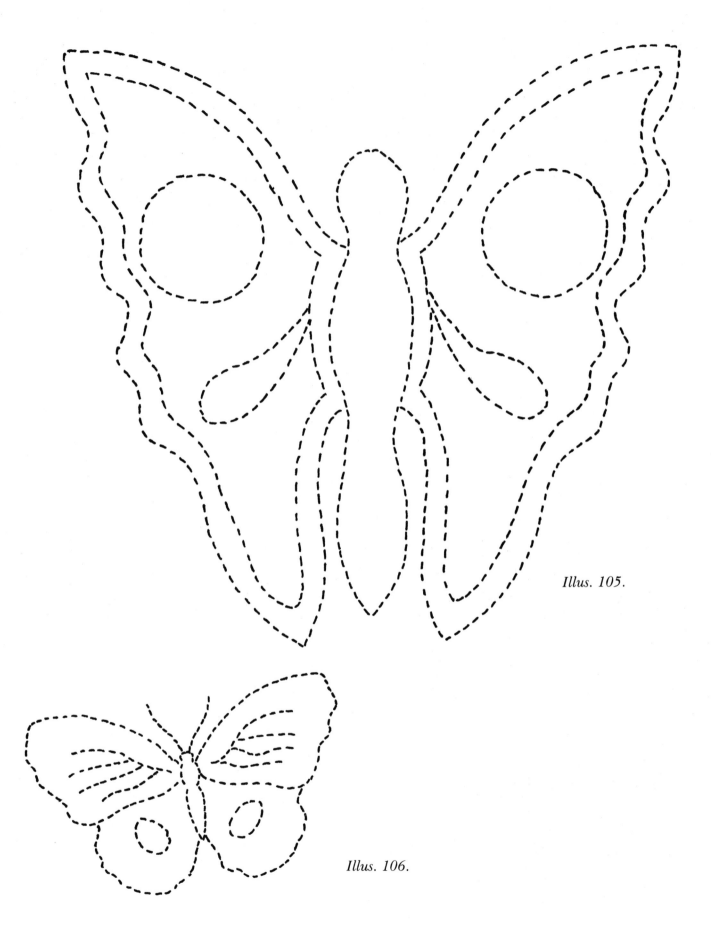

Illus. 105.

Illus. 106.

Illus. 107.

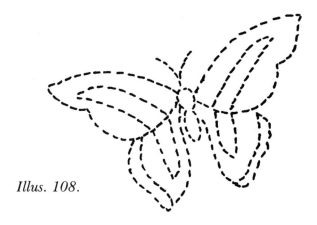

Illus. 108.

Illus. 109.

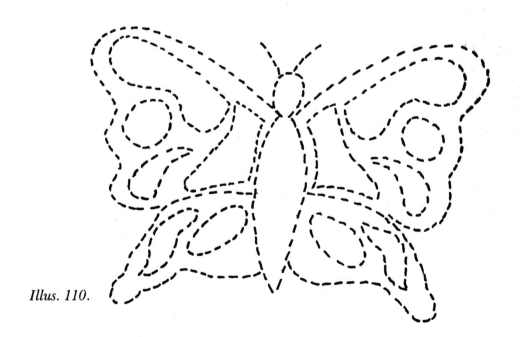

Illus. 110.

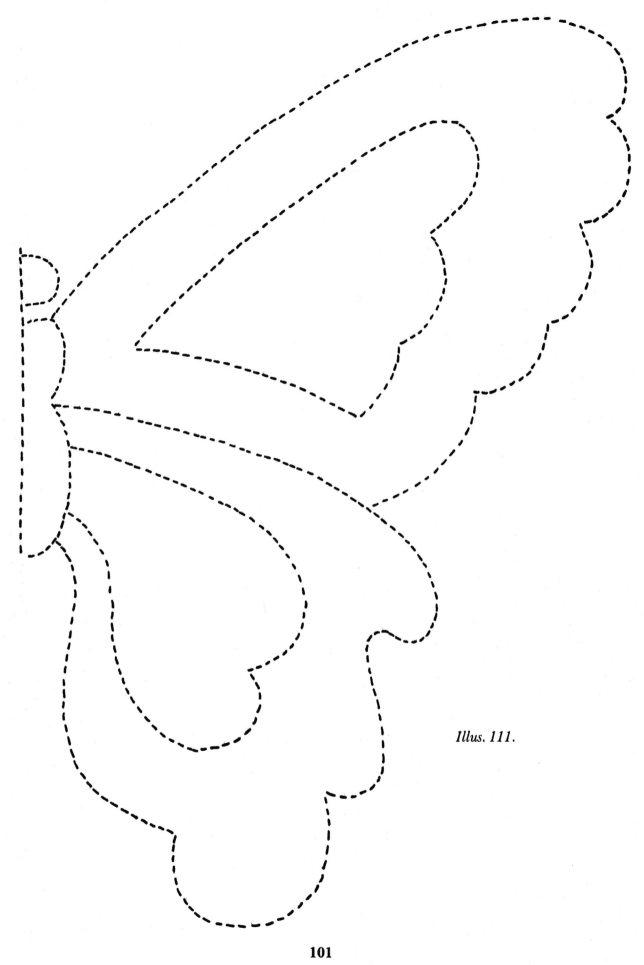

Illus. 111.

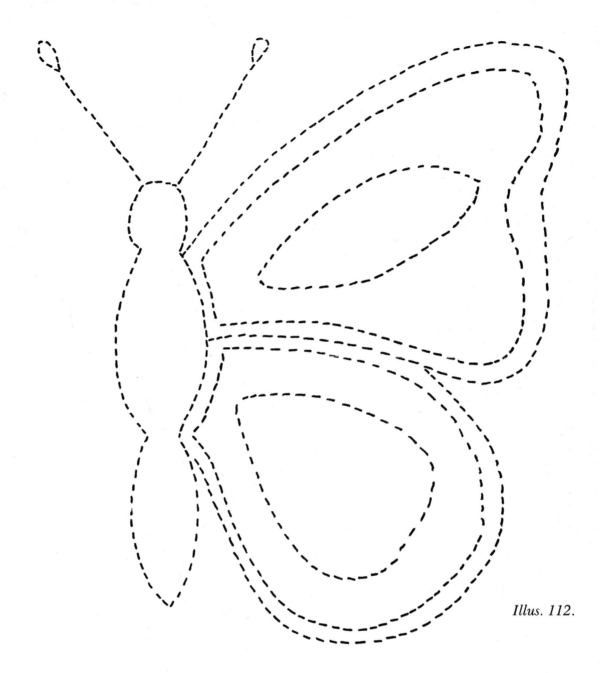

Illus. 112.

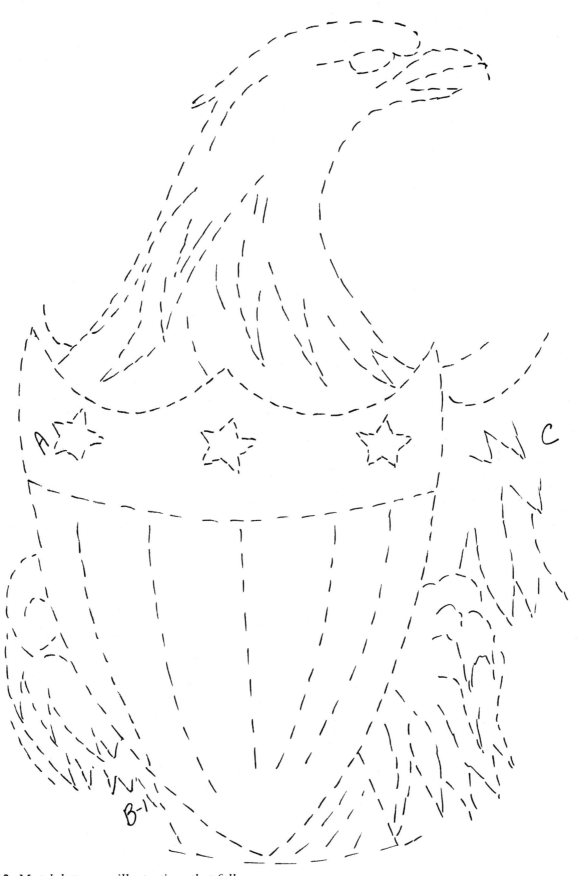

Illus. 113. Match letters on illustrations that follow.

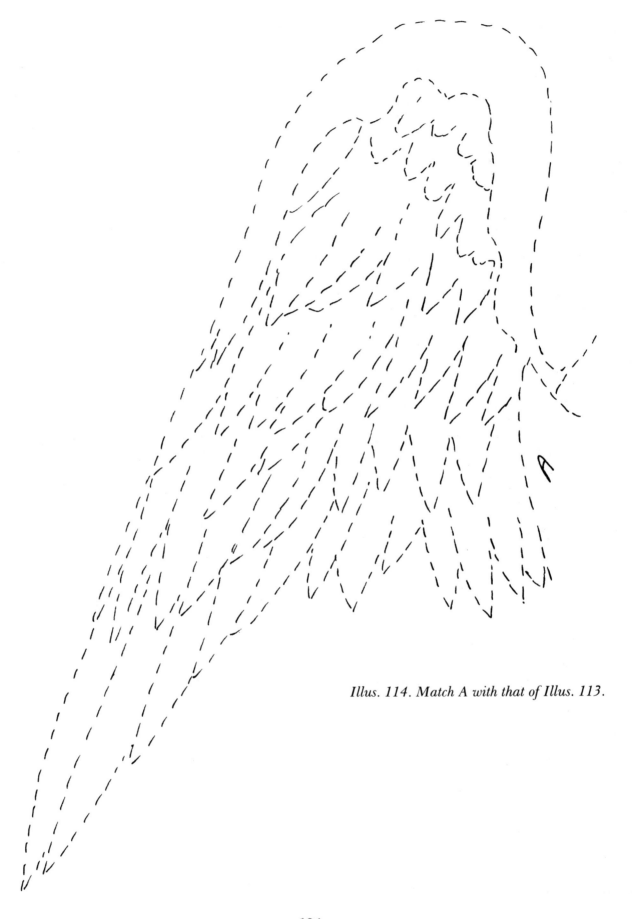

Illus. 114. Match A with that of Illus. 113.

Illus. 115. Match letters C and C-1.

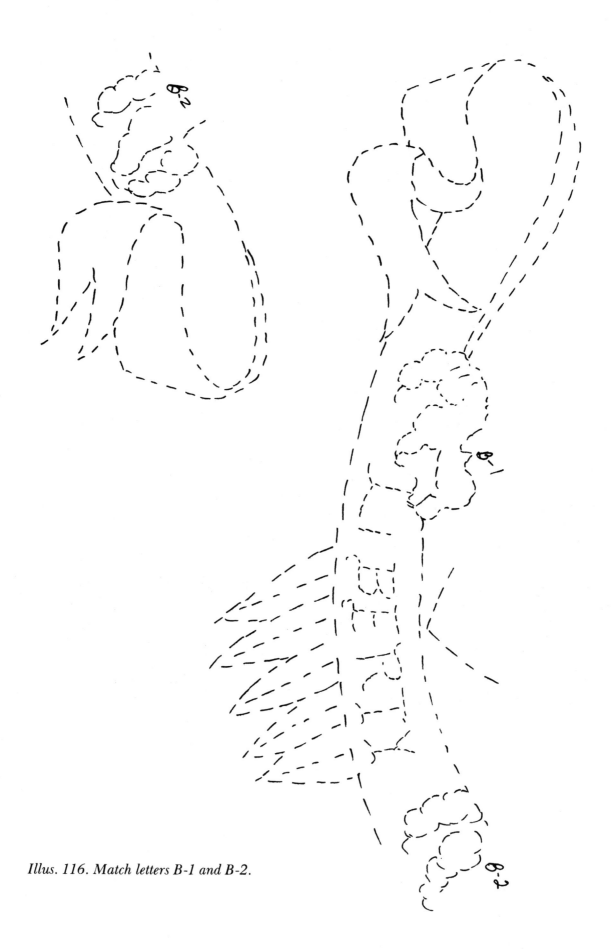

Illus. 116. Match letters B-1 and B-2.

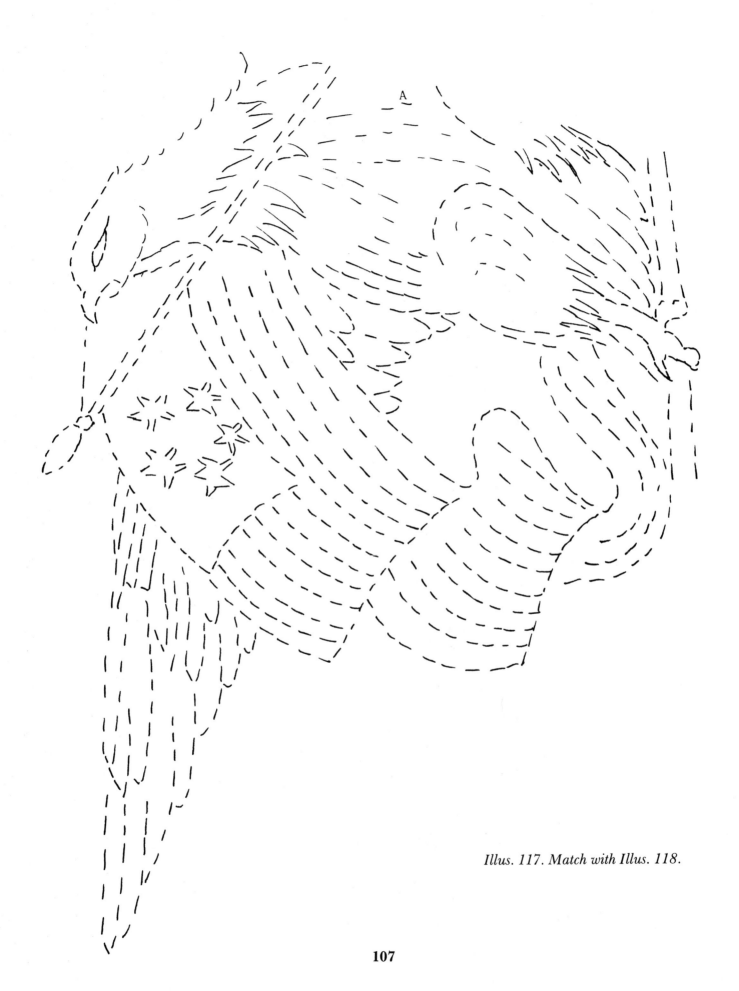

Illus. 117. Match with Illus. 118.

A

Illus. 118.

DESIGNS FOR CHILDREN

Illus. 119.

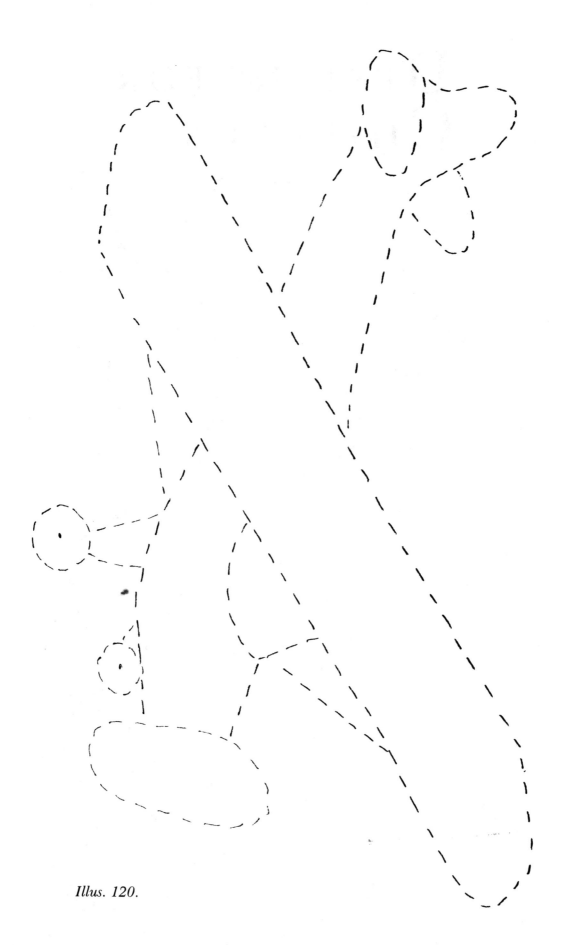

Illus. 120.

Illus. 121.

Illus. 122.

Illus. 123.

Illus. 124.

Illus. 125.

Illus. 126.

Illus. 127.

Illus. 128.

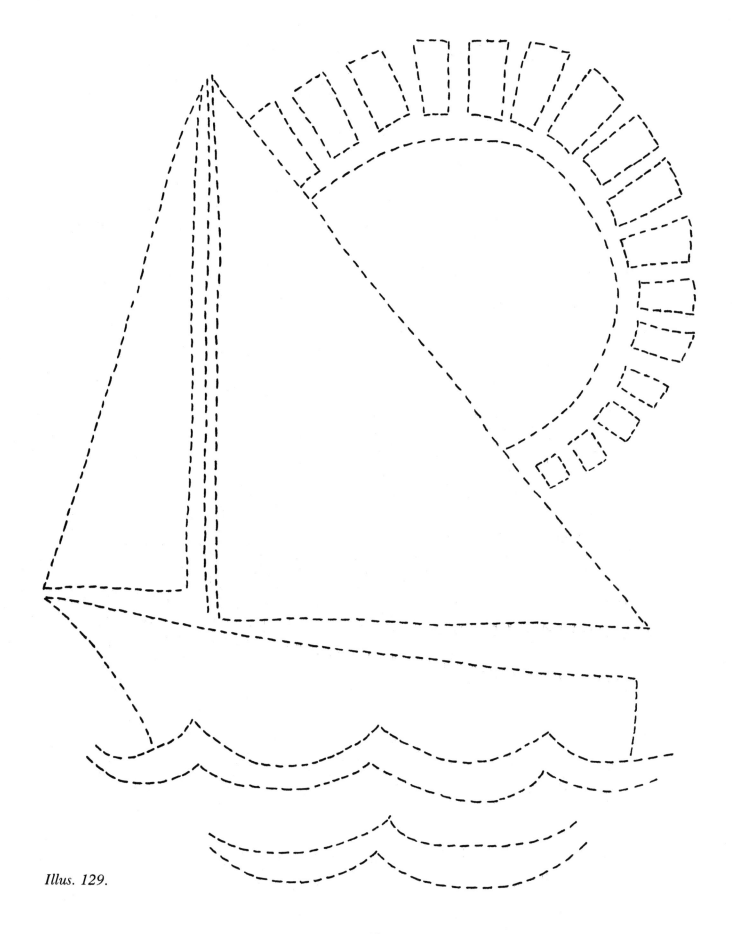

Illus. 129.

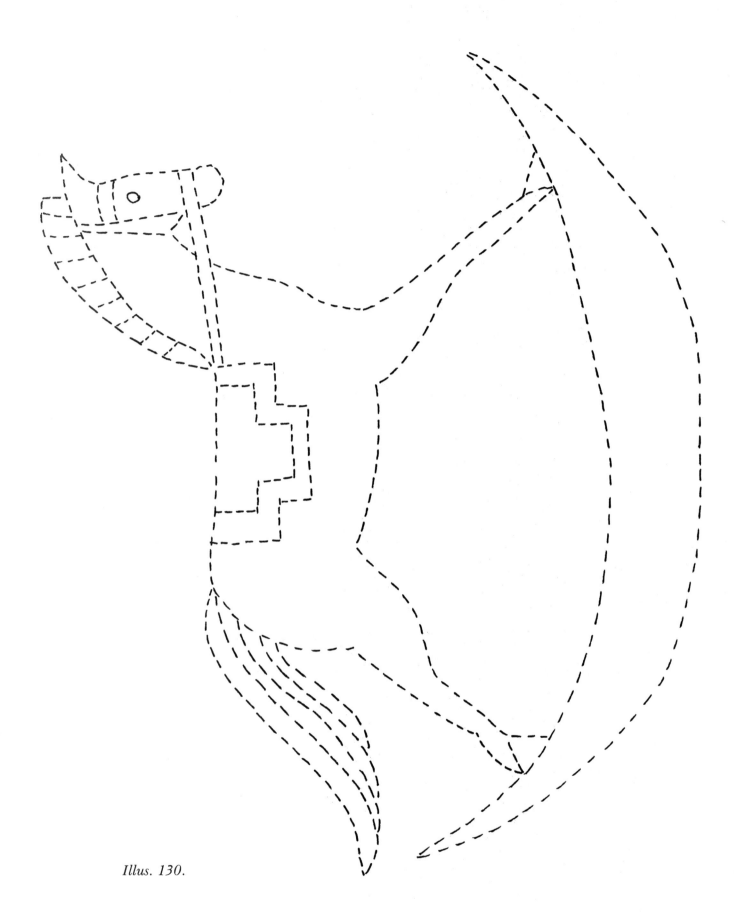

Illus. 130.

Illus. 131.

BORDERS

Illus. 132.

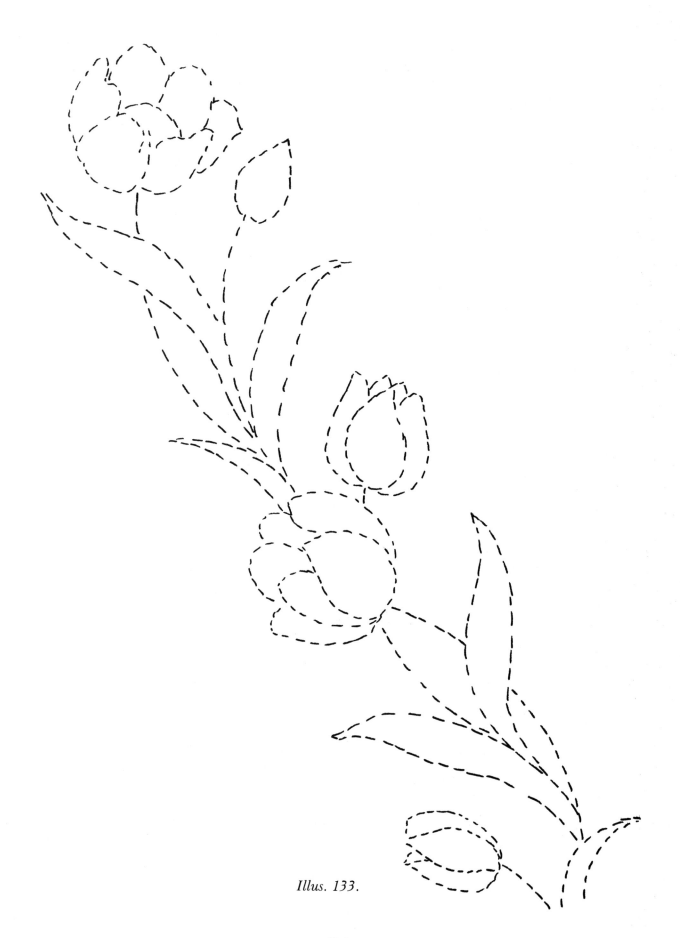

Illus. 133.

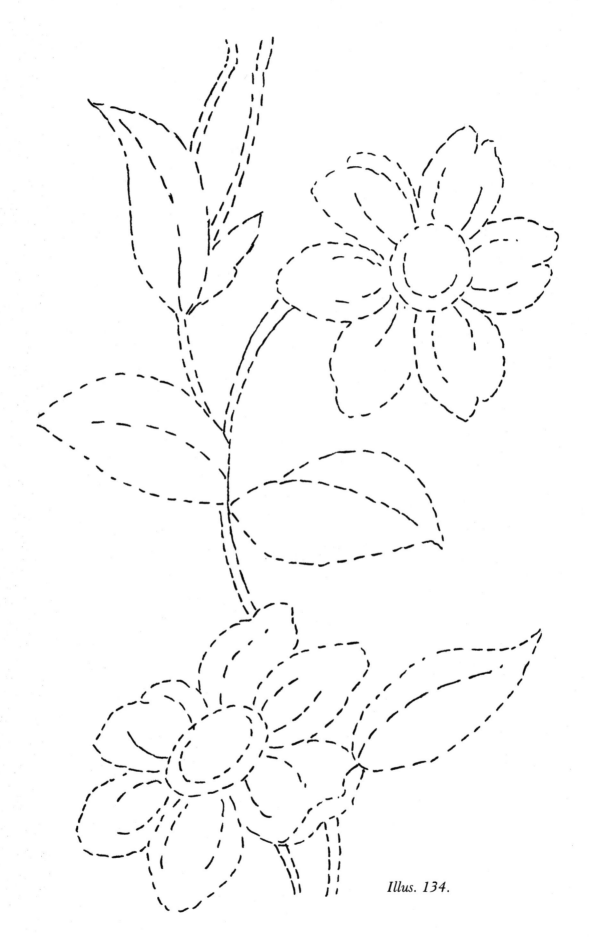

Illus. 134.

Illus. 135.

Illus. 136.

Illus. 137.   *Illus. 138.*

128

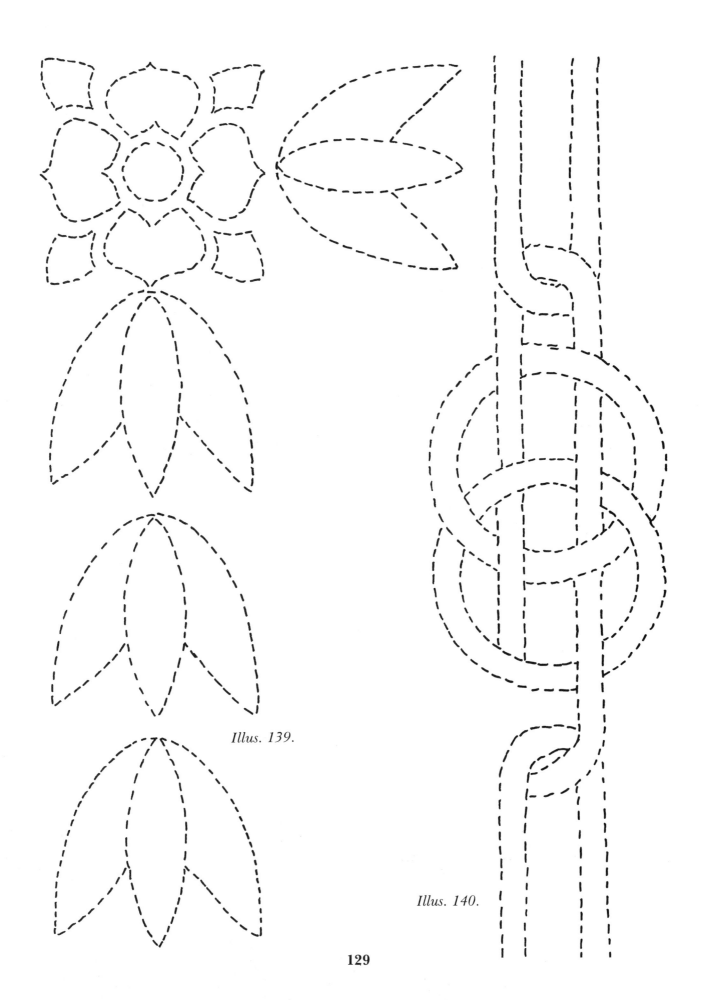

Illus. 139.

Illus. 140.

129

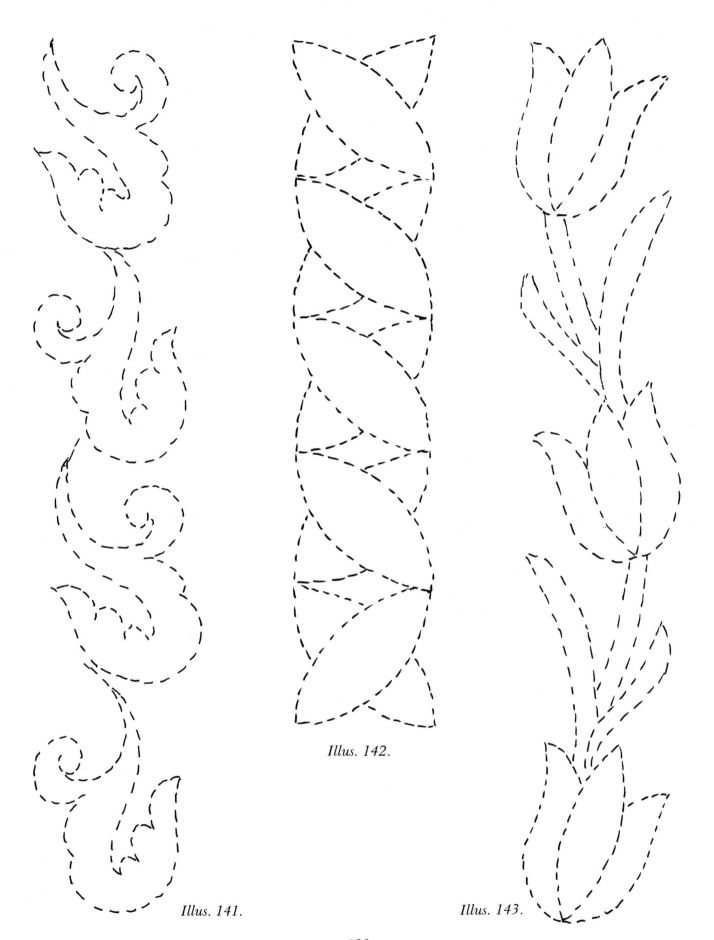

Illus. 141.

Illus. 142.

Illus. 143.

130

Illus. 144.   *Illus. 145.*   *Illus. 146.*

131

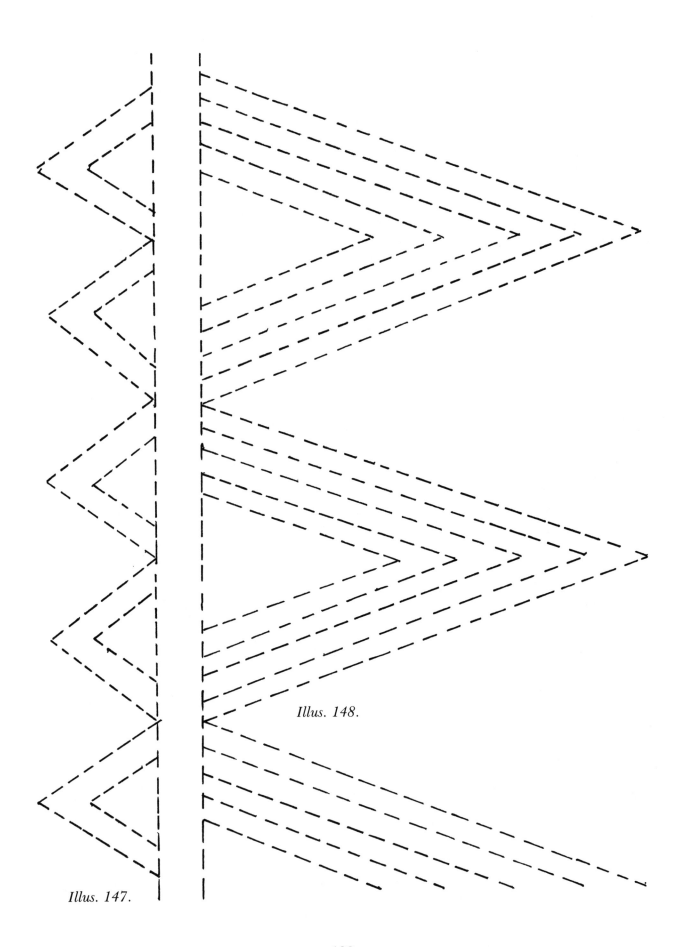

Illus. 148.

Illus. 147.

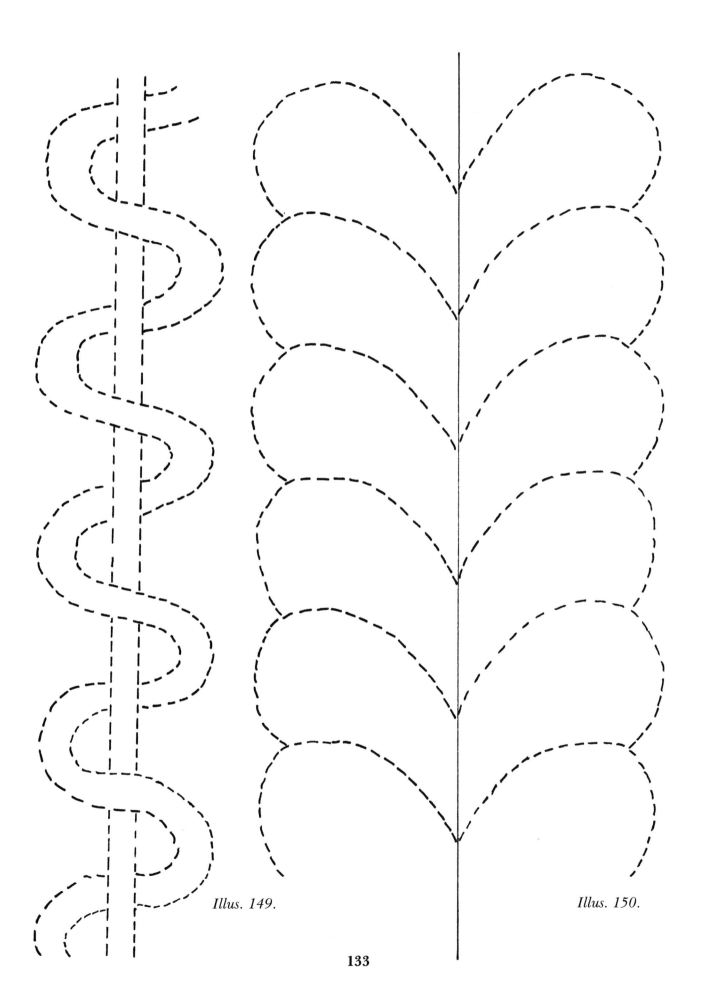

Illus. 149.

Illus. 150.

133

Illus. 151.

Illus. 152.

Illus. 153.

136

Illus. 154.

Illus. 155.

138

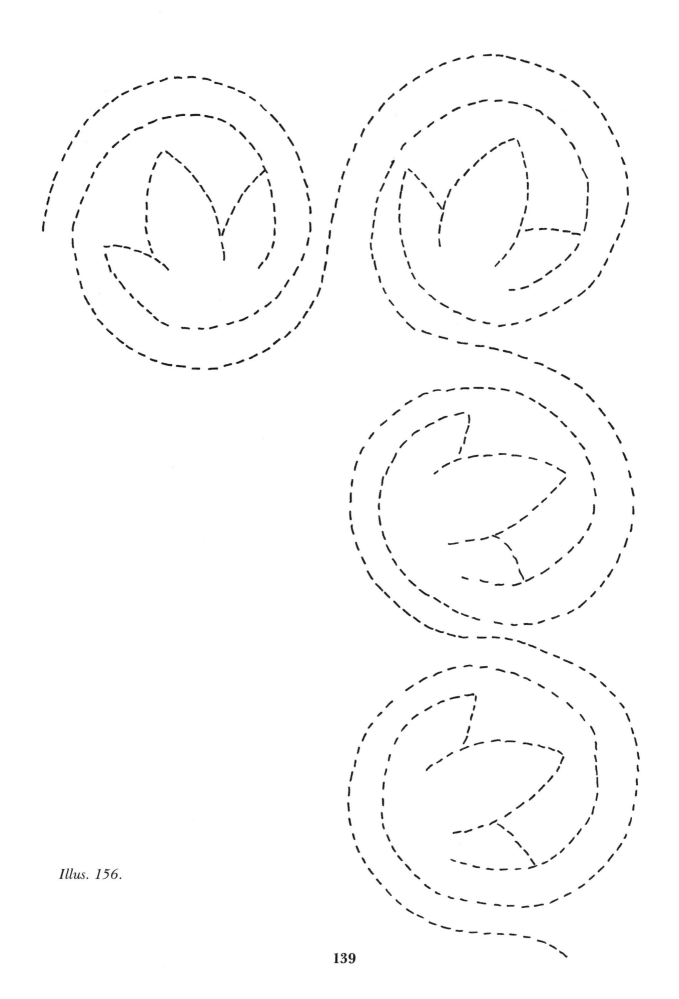

Illus. 156.

Illus. 157.

Illus. 158.

Illus. 159.

Illus. 160.   *Illus. 161.*

143

A

Illus. 162. Repeat pattern after joining A to A.

A

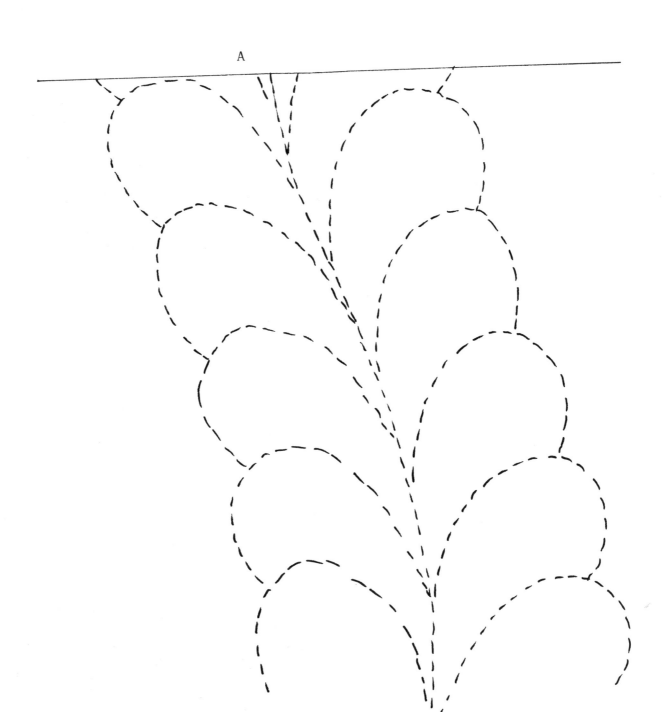

Illus. 163.

145

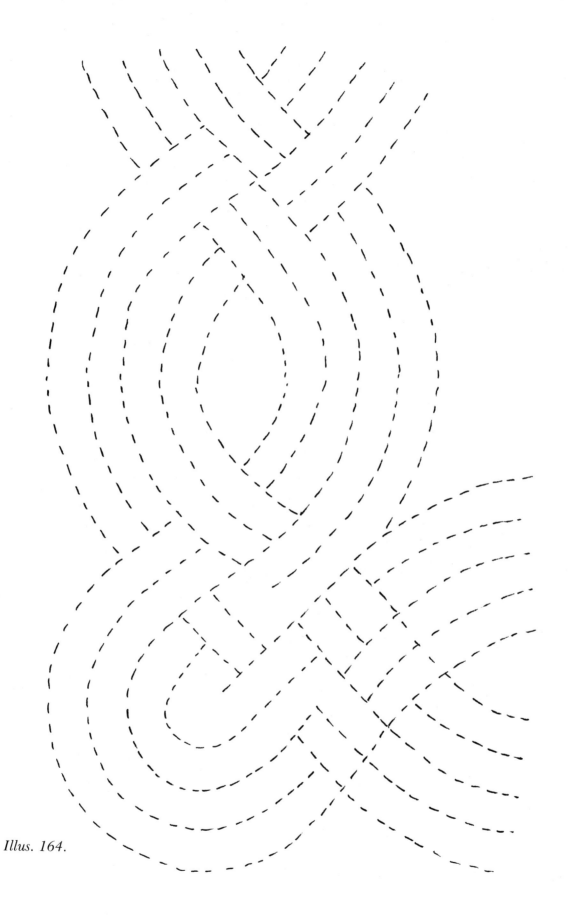

Illus. 164.

A

Illus. 165. Match with next two illustrations.

147

Illus. 166.

148

Illus. 167.

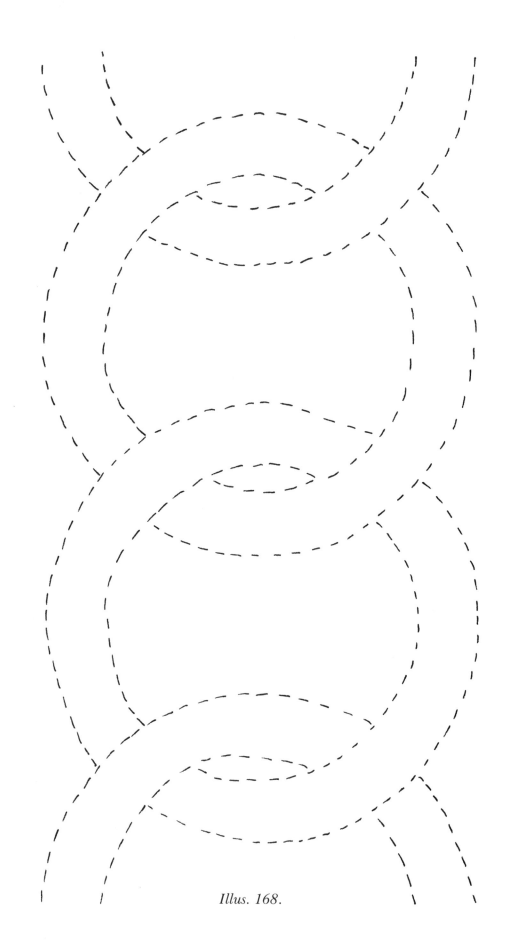

Illus. 168.

150

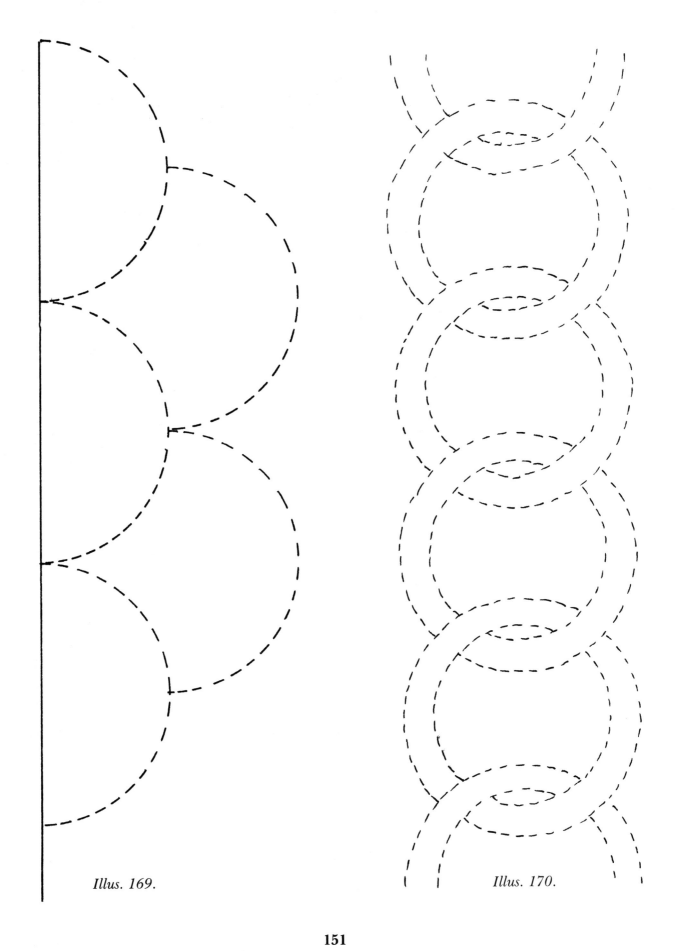

Illus. 169.

Illus. 170.

151

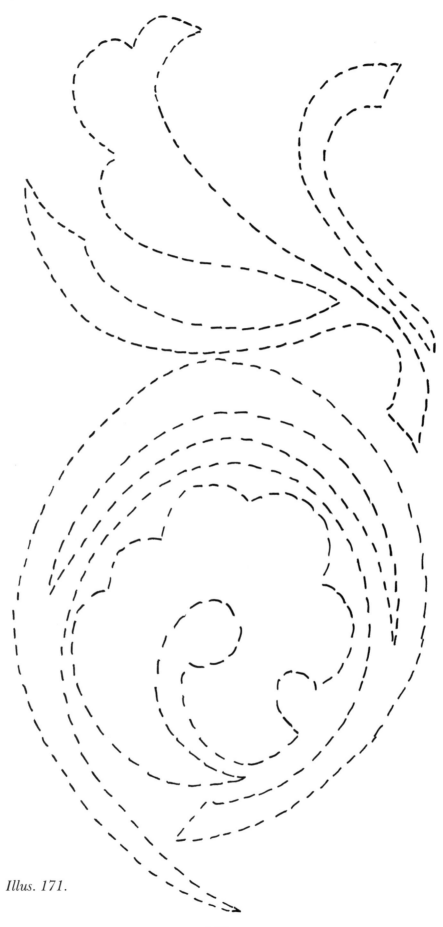

Illus. 171.

152

Illus. 172.   *Illus. 173.*

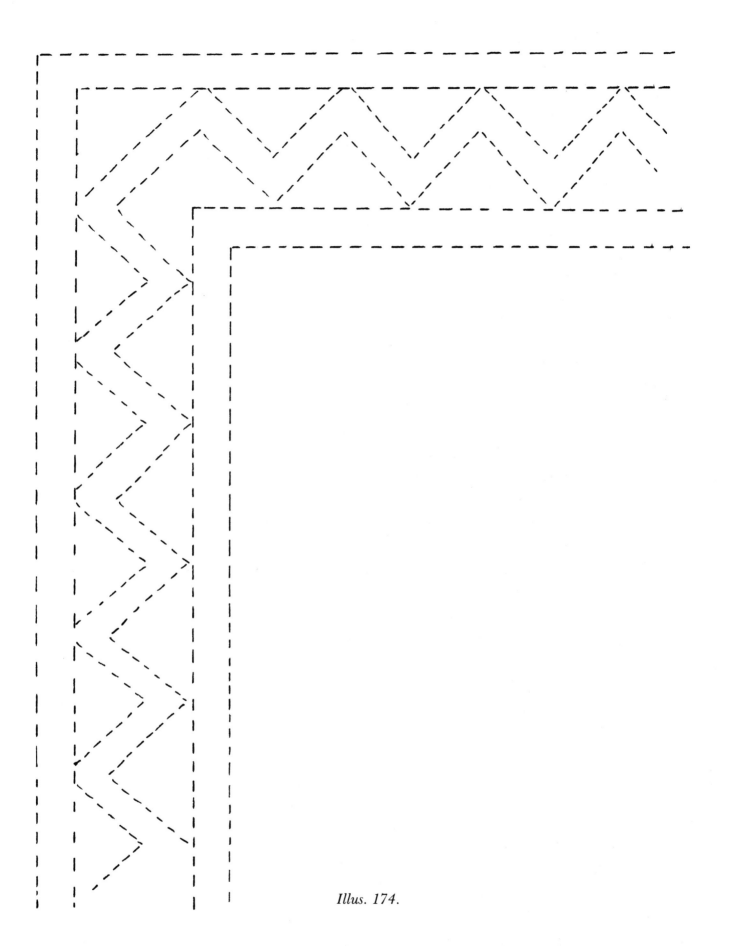

Illus. 174.

154

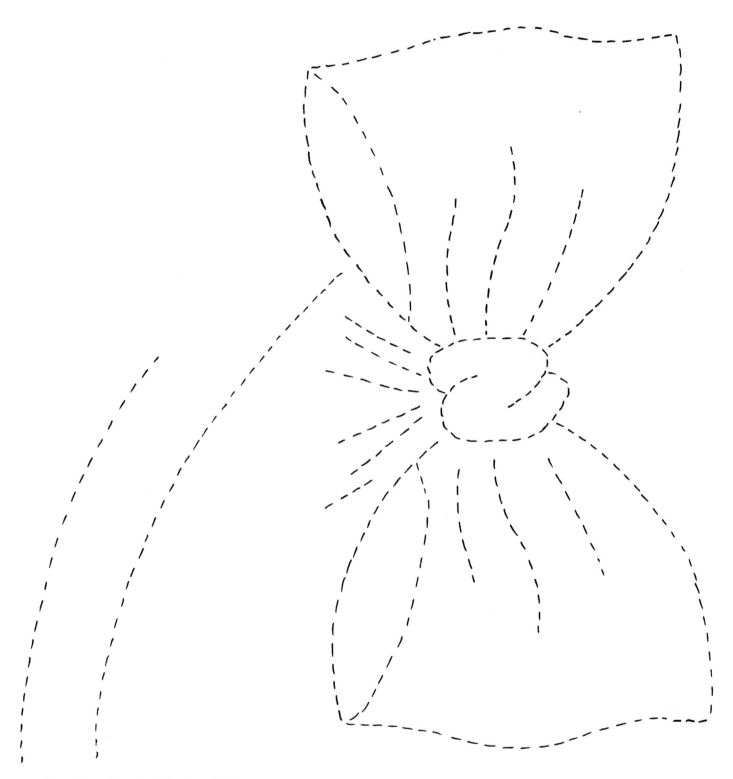

Illus. 176. Match with Illus. 177.

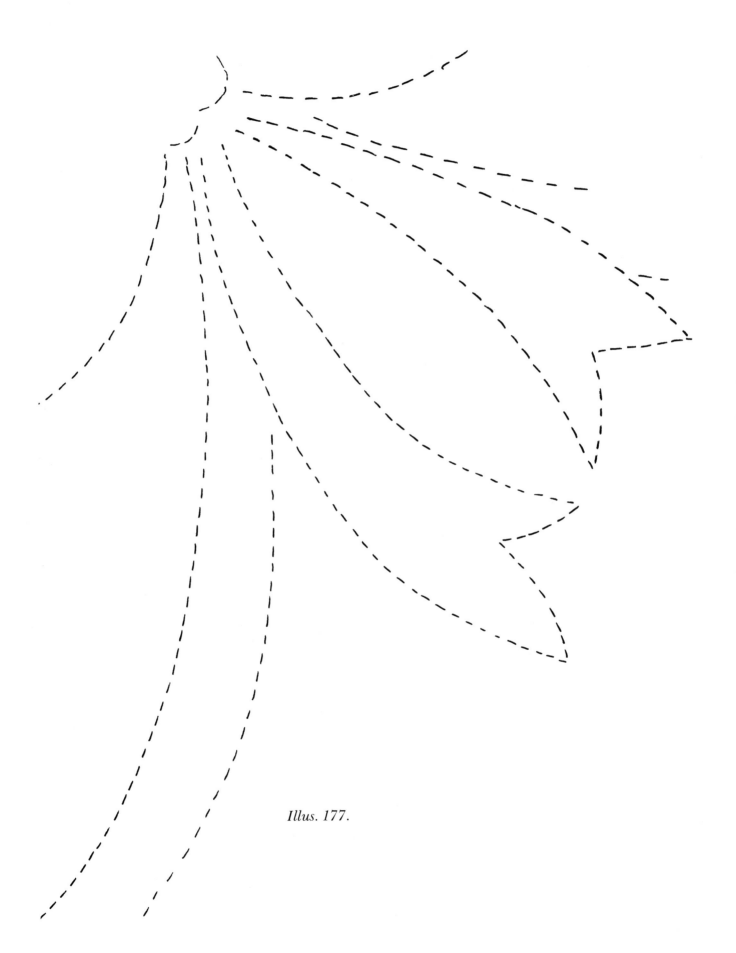

Illus. 177.

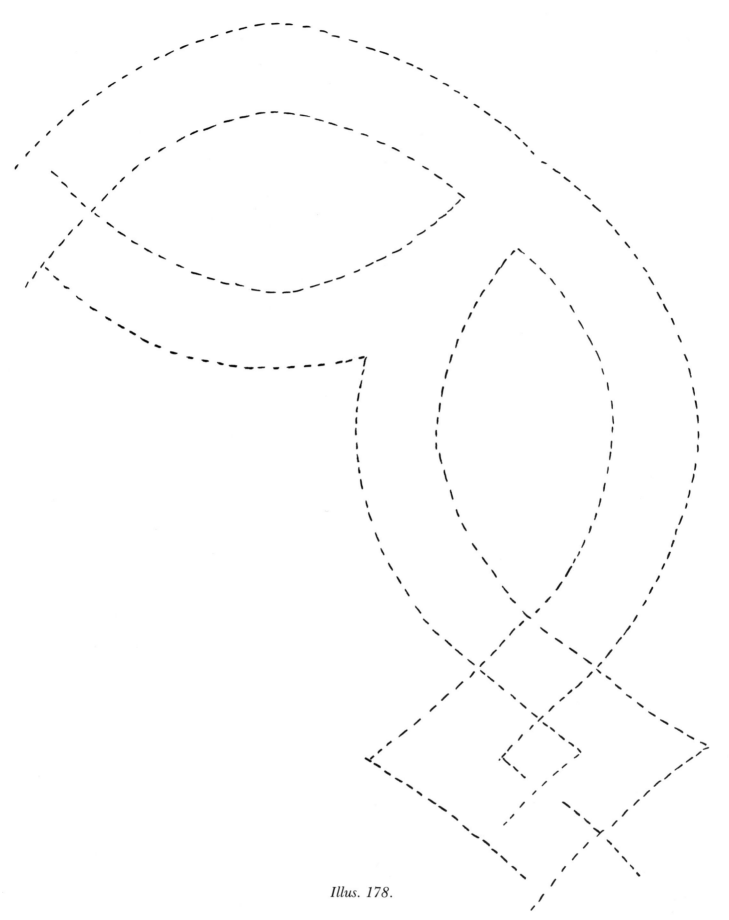

Illus. 178.

158

Illus. 179.

Illus. 180.

INDEX